Fostering **Mindfulness**

Building skills that students need to manage their attention, emotions,
and behavior in classrooms and beyond

Shelley Murphy

Pembroke Publishers Limited

Dedicated to the memories of Rob Greenhaigh and David Booth

© **2019 Pembroke Publishers**
538 Hood Road
Markham, Ontario, Canada L3R 3K9
www.pembrokepublishers.com

Distributed in the U.S. by Stenhouse Publishers
www.stenhouse.com

Funded by the Government of Canada
Financé par le gouvernement du Canada | Canada

Library and Archives Canada Cataloguing in Publication

Murphy, Shelley (Shelley Leigh), author
   Fostering mindfulness : building skills that students need to manage their attention, emotions, and behavior in classrooms and beyond / Shelley Murphy.

Includes bibliographical references and index.
Issued in print and electronic formats.
ISBN 978-1-55138-340-8 (softcover).--ISBN 978-1-55138-940-0 (PDF)

   1. Mindfulness (Psychology)--Study and teaching (Elementary). 2. Emotional intelligence--Study and teaching (Elementary). 3. Affective education. 4. Emotions and cognition. I. Title.

LB1072.M87 2019   370.15'34   C2018-905904-4
                                    C2018-905905-2

Editor: Kat Mototsune
Cover Design: John Zehethofer
Typesetting: Jay Tee Graphics Ltd.

Printed and bound in Canada
9 8 7 6 5 4 3 2 1

Contents

Introduction

Imagine a third-grade classroom. It is morning and students begin to arrive with the hustle and bustle that typically precedes the start of their school day. Dante skips through the door. He is talking from the moment he enters, providing a running commentary on everything he sees. Dante has a hard time "making thoughts in my head stop," as he puts it. When we all take our seats, his wide eyes fix on the bell at the front of the class. I can almost see his thoughts easing toward a less obtrusive stream. We are now months into the school year and, as always, each day begins and ends with a brief mindfulness practice. Dante and his classmates know this and ready themselves for the sound of the bell. At its signal, they are invited to participate in a brief mindful breathing exercise that asks them to become increasingly more present through focusing their awareness on their breath.

Most eyes are closed and students' attention is focused on noticing their own in-breath and out-breath. With hands on bellies, they ride the waves of their own breathing. As I look around the room, I see shoulders gradually dropping, the loosening of tense jaws, and faces softening. Quick and shallow breaths have converted to slower and deeper breathing—a sign that bodies and minds have moved into a more relaxed state. There seems to have been a palpable shift to presence and calm in the room. These few moments have been a welcome and calming refuge for all of us. They are also teaching valuable lessons in how to manage the demands of school and everyday life. After just a few moments, I ring the bell to signal the end of our practice. Students open their eyes and ready themselves for our literacy learning block. And so the day goes.

Dante and the rest of his class have come to expect and look forward to brief mindfulness lessons, activities, and practices as part of their school day. I have noticed, as many of them have, that they are becoming increasingly more able to manage their thoughts, attention, behaviors, and emotional responses. They are less restless and more easily able to deal with classroom stimulation, distraction and conflict. They are kinder to themselves and each other. In general, they are more focused, less reactive, and more at peace. Parents have noticed this too. Dante and the rest of his classmates will continue to spend a few minutes each day learning how to be more mindfully aware. They are learning how to manage their own thinking, attention, behaviors, and emotions, and are being given the tools to do so.

I first learned about mindfulness in the late '90s, while working as an early career elementary teacher in the heart of San Francisco. I was introduced to a Mindfulness Based Stress Reduction (MBSR) program (Kabat-Zinn, 2013) started by Jon Kabat-Zinn, Professor Emeritus of Medicine at the University of Massachusetts. After beginning to reap the personal benefits of mindfulness myself, I was motivated to try a few practices with Dante and the rest of my students. Fast forward a few decades: I continue to have a dedicated daily practice that has positively influenced every aspect of my life. As a mindfulness educator, I teach educators, parents, principals, administrators, teacher educators, graduate students, and teacher candidates how to embody and teach mindfulness practice.

Over the past 25 years, I have witnessed the ever-growing complexity and demands of the profession. As teachers, we are being called upon to support an increasingly diverse student population with varied strengths, challenges, and ways of being, knowing, and learning. The demands placed on our students have also changed. Studies show that today's children are experiencing a rising level of stress and worry that is alarmingly persistent and pervasive. They are also navigating a complex, fast-paced digital world that is a strong competing force for their attention, in the classroom and beyond. This seemingly magnetic pull toward their digital devices and social media, and the levels of stress they are experiencing, act as barriers to engagement, learning, and well-being. Teachers know this and are coming to understand the importance of giving students opportunities to learn how to strengthen their self-regulation skills, social emotional competencies, and ability to manage stress. This learning is as important as literacy and numeracy skills; it is foundational for successful learning and well-being.

Perhaps this is why interest in bringing mindfulness practice into educational settings has grown so rapidly in the last decade. Universities and K–12 schools across the globe are finding ways to incorporate mindfulness programs and practices into their regular schedules. The Ontario Institute for Studies in Education at the University of Toronto, where I am a teacher educator in the Department of Curriculum Teaching and Learning, has recently introduced opportunities for mindfulness education and practice to our entire community, in order to support mental health and well-being. Schools are responding because there is a mounting depth and breadth of scientific research being published on its benefits.

I have written this book for those of you in the educational field who are interested in deepening your understanding about mindfulness and its role in the classroom. It will help you incorporate simple and effective mindfulness lessons and activities that can help students cultivate the skills they need to support self-regulation, emotional well-being, and learning. Perhaps you will find, as so many of us have, that mindfulness practices encourage children to more mindfully and heartfully respond to their inner and outer experiences of the world and to the experiences of others. Through brief daily activities, students can learn to meet each moment of their school day (and beyond) with greater awareness, attention, and resilience. This ultimately helps prepare them for learning and for life.

Using This Book

This book will help you build mindfulness skills in the classroom through simple, creative, ready-to-use lessons. Step-by-step lessons can be easily and immediately integrated into your school day and adapted for diverse classrooms. Scripts accompany many of the lessons; they are offered only as suggested guides. They should be modified to fit your particular needs and the diverse needs of your students. Most importantly, they should reflect a depth of understanding that comes from your own practice.

This book is not meant to be used as a prescribed curriculum or program. If you are experienced in bringing mindfulness practices to your students, you may choose to use this book as a way to enhance your already-existing program. In this case you might find it most helpful to jump around through the chapters to sample some of the skill-building exercises that might be new to you and your students, and that apply to your particular setting.

If you are embarking on bringing mindfulness into your classroom for the first time, Chapters 1 to 3 can be used as a somewhat chronological overview. These chapters offer the building blocks for introducing, teaching, and leading mindfulness in your classroom. Once you have laid the foundation for mindfulness, you will find many lessons to choose from in the remaining chapters of the book. Please consider what resonates with you and applies to your setting and your students.

In Chapters 2 though 8, you will find lessons that include step-by-step instructions and guiding scripts. You will find practical reproducible templates and activity sheets, as well as illustrative photos and text written by practicing teachers to share their experiences of implementing particular mindfulness practices into their school day.

Chapter 1: Why Mindfulness Matters in the Classroom explores what mindfulness is, presents common myths, and explains the science behind how mindfulness helps support emotion, behavior, and attention regulation.

Chapter 2: Getting Started provides suggestions for how to prepare yourself and your learning environment for mindfulness practice. It includes sample letters to parents and two starter lessons for introducing mindfulness to students. These lessons help set the stage for mindful breathing (Chapter 3) and the remaining activities and practices throughout the book.

Chapter 3: Mindful Breathing introduces a core mindfulness practice that is foundational to all mindfulness practices. It explains what mindful breathing is and the rationale for students practicing it. It includes various lessons for introducing activities to help your students become aware of and learn about their breath. The remaining activities give you an opportunity to guide your students through various fun and engaging mindful breathing exercises.

Chapter 4: Mindfulness and the Five Senses includes various lessons to help students use their senses (smell, hearing, touch, taste, and sight) as anchors for mindfulness practice.

Chapter 5: Mindfulness of Emotions introduces mindfulness and the ABCs of the brain, and various lessons and activities to help students learn how to recognize, name, and manage their emotions.

Chapter 6: Mindful Movement includes mindful movement games and activities, including yoga, to help students bring awareness to the connection between their bodies and their minds.

Once you and your students are familiar with a particular activity, you may bypass the introductory steps and dive straight into the practice.

Chapter 7: Guided Mindfulness includes several guided mindfulness and guided imagery activities to give students opportunities to use their imaginations and awareness to practice focusing their attention and being in the moment.

Chapter 8: Mindfulness and the Peace Corner includes suggestions and ideas for how to introduce, set up, and manage a Peace Corner to give students opportunities to engage in practicing self-regulation and self-care.

May the lessons within this book help you foster mindfulness for yourself and for your students in the classroom and beyond.

Acknowledgments

I have many wonderful people in my life to thank for what I have learned, practiced, and taught, and for helping me to bring this book to life.

I am very grateful to Mary Macchiusi for believing in this book and for being such an amazing support through the various stages of publication. I am indebted to my editor Kat Mototsune for shepherding this work so beautifully from start to finish.

As this book is culled from years of learning experiences and practice, I would like to acknowledge a few of the people whose profound influence shines through its pages. My deepest thanks to Jon Kabat-Zinn, Jack Miller, Thich Nhat Hanh, Jack Kornfield, and Elizabeth Cotton. Thank you to OISE colleagues and students who continue to create an environment that supports inquiry, reflection, and growth. I wish to thank Brenda Stein Dzaldov, Linda Cameron, Clare Kosnik, and Clive Beck for ushering me toward writing this book. Grateful acknowledgment is made to my students, past and present, the most recent of whom are future or practicing teachers. You kindle the flame of my continued learning. A heartfelt thank you to the incredible teachers whose stories from the classroom permeate this book, and to anyone who teaches, leads, and/or practices mindfulness. You help make the world a better place.

I am eternally grateful to the memory of David Booth, who was my mentor, colleague, and dear friend. David championed the Pembroke author in me, and was a pillar in my life and in the lives of so many. A special note of deep gratitude to the memory of Rob Greenhalgh, who was my friend since elementary school and whose influence on my life is indelible. He envisioned this book and inspired me to write it.

I wish to thank Bill Young, a touchstone and wordsmith whose encouragement and feedback through the decades helped me to become a teacher, academic, and writer. Thank you to Susan Hammond, Dana Chapman, Jacqueline Gervais, Monica McGlynn-Stewart, and Bev Swerling for their friendship and encouragement along the way. Thank you also to Sam Gardner for his wit, imagination, and diligent support. A special thank you to Cynthia Somai, whose creative insights and unwavering assistance helped guide this book to completion. It would not have reached its full potential without her.

Without my family this book would not be before you. Thank you to my sister Cheryl for being both a mirror and a window, and for her many insights and discerning editorial feedback. A debt of thanks to my mom Dorothy Murphy, whose endless energy and joy fuel me. Thank you to my twin brother Shawn for his positive nature and affirming encouragement that ground me beyond measure. I thank my sister-in-law Kathy Teed, my brother-in-law Dave Robinson, my nieces

Danielle and Megan Murphy, my nephews Noah, Mason, and Ben Robinson, and the memory of my father James Murphy. My expression of gratitude for their strength, humor, and support could take up another book.

Finally, thank you to Rich Goldstein for being beside me for the writing of this book and for taking the journey with me through life. How much sweeter it all is because of you.

Illustration Credits

1

Why Mindfulness Matters in the Classroom

What Is Mindfulness?

Mindfulness is both a way of being in the world and a practice. As a way of being, mindfulness is the quality of presence we bring to everything we do. It describes our innate capacity to pay full and conscious attention to something in the moment. It is the awareness that emerges from paying attention on purpose, in the present moment, and nonjudgmentally to the unfolding of our experience (Kabat-Zinn, 2013).

Each of us naturally experiences states of mindfulness. Think of being in nature and hiking to the peak of a beautiful mountain. When you are completely attentive to where you are and what you are experiencing as you make your way to the summit, you are in a state of mindfulness. You may feel the rise and fall of the path beneath your feet or notice the majesty of the trees, the curve of a stream, or the calls of wildlife as you climb. This present awareness is an experience of mindfulness. You are not experiencing mindfulness if you are in the midst of hiking and your mind is elsewhere. The *elsewhere* is often described as "mindlessness" or "being on autopilot." This is when our bodies are in one place but our thoughts are somewhere else. Many of us have had the experience of driving in a car to get from one place to another and having had very little or no awareness or recollection of what we passed along the way. Our bodies were in the car getting us from point A to point B, but our minds, for the most part, were elsewhere. While we were focused enough on our driving and the environment around us to get to our destinations safely, our attention was being distracted by the endless stream of thoughts in our head.

Our brains are fantastic time-travel machines. We spend a lot of time thinking about the past and plenty of time thinking and worrying about the future. In other words, we spend a lot of time thinking about what is not happening in the moment.

A recent Harvard study showed that our minds wander 47% of the time (Killingsworth & Gilbert, 2010). This means we are spending almost half of our waking hours thinking and worrying about something other than what we are actually doing. Our brains are in a default mode of mind wandering and are, in essence, being perpetually hijacked.

While mindfulness is an innate capacity we all naturally possess, it is also more readily available to us when we practice on a daily basis. In this sense, it is helpful to think of mindfulness as a skill that can be cultivated and strengthened over time through various formal and informal exercises. We recognize the importance of exercising our bodies to help keep them healthy, resilient, and strong. In the same way, our minds require attention and exercise to keep them healthy, resilient, and strong. Think of mindfulness as mental strength training for your students' brains. Like a workout for their bodies, it takes regular practice and some discipline.

Here is how the practice of mindfulness works. Mindfulness practice is often defined as the intentional focusing of our awareness on our thoughts, our feelings, our body sensations, and the surrounding environment without judging them. It typically involves directing attention to a specific focus, often called an *anchor*, such as the breath. I invite you to experiment with this for a moment. Shift your attention away from reading this book to focus solely on your breathing. Close your eyes and just notice your in-breath and your out-breath for one minute. Then come back to reading where you left off.

It is important to be gentle and kind to a wandering mind during mindfulness practice.

Chances are, within a very short period of time, your mind was drawn away to thoughts, sounds, or physical sensations. Actually, this is the nature of our minds; it is typical and expected. Despite this, people most often give up on mindfulness practice because they think they are doing it wrong when their minds wander repeatedly. In fact, it is when you realize your mind has wandered and you bring your attention back to your breath that you are experiencing, practicing, and strengthening mindfulness. It is the repeated redirection of the mind back to focusing on the anchor that breaks the conditioned response of distraction. It also strengthens the part of the brain that controls self-regulation and promotes greater resilience and a variety of positive mental and physical outcomes.

Common Myths about Mindfulness

As mindfulness increases in popularity, misconceptions, myths, and confusions abound. Here are a few things to consider:

- Myth: *Mindfulness practice is a religion.* While mindfulness has its roots in many cultures, philosophies, religions, and psychologies, it is a universal practice that is now most widely considered secular or mainstream. Secular mindfulness exercises were brought to the mainstream, in part, through the work of Jon Kabat-Zinn. The mindfulness exercises, lessons, and practices introduced in this book are not connected, in any way, to religious or spiritual practice. They are life-skill practices designed to help students develop habits of mind central to learning, resilience, and well-being.
- Myth: *Mindfulness is about clearing the mind.* In fact, it is quite the opposite. In mindfulness practices, we give our students' minds something to focus on. Thoughts will actually come and go, and this is part of the practice. Mindfulness is about becoming a witness to those thoughts without being drawn into them. It is not about making thoughts stop. It is about simply noticing them.
- Myth: *Mindfulness requires a lot of time.* Daily practice is important, but it does not take a lot of time from the school day. When you engage your students in as little as 10 minutes a day of regular practice, you are giving

them the opportunity to become more skilled in how they regulate their emotions, attention, impulses, and responses.

- Myth: *Mindfulness requires a quiet space to practice.* While it is ideal to have as quiet an environment as possible during mindfulness practice, it is not entirely necessary. Schools and classrooms are full of expected and unexpected movement, noise, and interruption. Mindfulness activities can be practiced in the midst of all of this. There is no need to wait for a "right" moment.
- Myth: *Mindfulness is not backed by scientific research.* There is a depth and breadth of research showing the ways in which mindfulness practices support attention, focus, and executive functioning (Leyland, Rowse, & Emerson. 2018); regulation of emotions and behavior (Black & Fernando, 2014; Schonert-Reichl et al., 2015; Semple et al., 2010); empathy and perspective-taking (MacDonald & Price, 2017; Schonert-Reichl et al., 2015); stress management (Schonert-Reichl et al., 2015; Sibinga et al., 2016); and overall academic performance and well-being (Brown & Ryan, 2003; Schonert-Reichl et al., 2015).

Self-Regulation and Emotions, Attention, and Behavior

For children to be successful in school and in life, they need to be able to manage their thoughts, emotions, attention, and behaviors during the rigors of the school day and beyond. This ability to self-manage is often called *self-regulation*. According to Stuart Shanker, a leading authority on self-regulation and child development, "we are in the midst of a revolution in educational thinking and practice. Scientific advances in a number of fields point to a similar argument—how well students do in school can be determined by how well they are able to self-regulate" (2013, p. IX). In fact, many studies have shown that self-regulation is more important than IQ when it comes to predicting a child's ability to do well in school.

So, what is self-regulation? Self-regulation, as a capacity of well-being, has been defined in a number of ways. It often gets confused with the idea of self-control or compliance; it is neither. In its most basic sense, it is a student's ability to effectively manage their attention, behaviors, and emotions in different situations. It is a skill set that allows them to develop strategies and habits of mind to help them achieve personal goals and respond mindfully to their everyday experiences:

- Emotion self-regulation is a student's ability to recognize and name what they are feeling at any given moment and the ability to calm themselves in the face of challenging emotions and stress.
- Attention self-regulation is a student's ability to focus and keep their attention where they want and need it to be, despite distraction.
- Behavior self-regulation is a student's ability to act in socially appropriate ways, to adapt to new situations, and to respond thoughtfully to impulses.

Mindfulness and Emotions

Emotional well-being is crucial to learning and life success. Research shows that children who are able to regulate their emotions are better at recognizing and

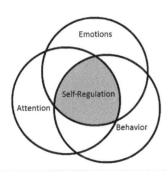

managing their feelings and behaviors, making informed decisions, empathizing with and being kind to others, and coping with challenges. Not surprisingly, they also do better in school (Goldman, 1995).

Students who have high levels of stress have a much more difficult time managing their emotions. If you ask most teachers, they will tell you they see an alarming increase in the number of students experiencing stress and anxiety in the classroom. This stress makes it hard for students to manage difficult feelings like anger, fear, or sadness, and it makes it difficult for them to learn. When our students are in a negative emotional state and are experiencing stress, there is a cascade of reactions that happens in their brains and bodies. Their thinking brains (prefrontal cortex) go temporarily offline in service of their survival brain (amygdala) (see image below).

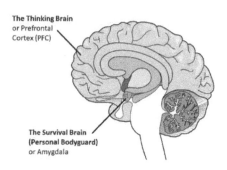

The amygdala is often called the *reptilian brain* or our *fight-flight-or-freeze* response.

The amygdala is one of the oldest parts of the brain and is consumed with survival. It is constantly scanning for threats or danger to avoid to help keep us safe. To help us flee or fight, our heart rate and blood pressure increase, our breath becomes quick and shallow, our pupils dilate, blood flow is sent to our arm and leg muscles and away from our internal organs, digestion shuts down because it is not immediately necessary for survival, and stress hormones course through our bloodstream. These responses are unconscious and automatic. All of this is in service of survival. The problem is that the amygdala cannot tell the difference between a true emergency and an imagined one. It can be triggered by a thought, a memory, or a worry about the future. These are not physical threats to us, but our brains experience them as though they are. So, in response, our bodies go into alert mode and our thinking brain (prefrontal cortex) temporarily shuts down. This stops us from thinking clearly. Over time, the amygdala grows and the brain gets used to responding to everyday life as though it is a threat. Executive functions, which are important for planning, problem-solving, and reasoning, are negatively affected. So it is very important for children to learn how to manage their stress response when it is not needed.

The good news is that mindfulness practice helps students do just that. Research shows regular mindfulness practice shrinks the amygdala, while the prefrontal cortex becomes stronger (Taren, Creswell, Gianaros, 2013). Teaching mindfulness to children helps them better identify, understand, and manage their emotions. This leads to improved learning and overall well-being.

Mindfulness and Attention

Attention is a first starting point of learning. The impact of our teaching is dependent on our students' ability to focus their minds at any given moment and to maintain that focus in the face of distraction. A student's ability to focus their attention is a predictor of school success. Of course, we know this is easier for some students and more challenging for others. The reality is that teachers are in competition for their students' attention. We are in an era of multitasking and distractibility in a new frontier of interactive technologies and digital media. Research shows that 8- to 12-year-olds spend, on average, anywhere from 4½ to 6 hours each day on forms of screen media. Many of us have wondered how this affects our students' developing brains. A recent longitudinal study appeared in Journal of the American Medical Association on the connection between children's media use and their ability to focus their attention. Researchers (Ra, et al., 2018) tracked 2500 teens over two years, monitoring how much they used digital media and what their symptoms were. They found the more adolescents use digital media, such as social media, texting, browsing, streaming, etc., the more they are at risk for developing the characteristics of ADHD; i.e., inattention and hyperactivity.

So what does all this research tell us? It tells us we need to pay attention to students' attention and give them opportunities to strengthen it. They are expected to focus as we try to engage them in learning, but we rarely teach them how to do this more effectively. Mindfulness is one way to train their brains to focus their attention where they want it to be and to keep it there. Research shows that regular mindfulness practice helps sharpen and strengthen attention and concentration skills to keep students focused on their learning (Black & Fernando, 2013; Costello, 2014). The more they practice, the more they will benefit.

Mindfulness and Behavior

When students struggle in their learning, we respond by gathering as much information as we can to better understand what the barrier to learning might be; we shift our approach in response; and we work to strengthen their confidence, motivation, and skills. When students struggle with behavior challenges, the response tends to be quite different. As Ross Greene, who has written widely on supporting children with behavior challenges, has said, "Kids do well if they can." He suggests, "Behind every challenging behavior is an unsolved problem or a lagging skill (or both)" (Greene, 2008). It makes sense for us to ask ourselves what a particular student's challenging behaviors might be telling us about what they need. Of course, for every child the answer will be somewhat different.

Self-regulation expert Stuart Shanker believes that many of our students are showing what he calls stress behaviors in the classroom (Shanker, 2012). These students are not fully aware of what they are doing or why, and might be limited in their ability to act differently. If children have been repeatedly exposed to highly stressful situations or trauma they tend to be hypervigilant, because their brains are wired to be on high alert for a perceived threat or danger. Feelings like fear and anger can be perceived by students' brains as threats and can trigger impulsive behaviors. These behaviors act almost like a defence to the stressful situation. All of this means that while students' brains are consumed with scanning and responding to perceived threats, there is little room for learning. So what are teachers to do? Shanker (2012) argues we need to help students develop the strategies they need to calm their nervous systems down when they are feeling afraid, angry, stressed, or agitated.

As you have read, mindfulness is a way to help students calm their nervous systems. Over time, this helps them come out of a default mode of stress. When difficult emotions, such as anger and fear, rise up, mindfulness practice helps

The fact that many major tech companies have developed special technology to help combat the addictive qualities of screen media is indicative of the level of concern about the connection between screen media and lack of attention.

students respond more thoughtfully and with more awareness. Mindfulness helps create some thoughtful space between an impulse and an action. This can mean the difference between a poor behavior response and a good one. Over time, this leads to positive behavior change.

Mindfulness is not a behavior-management technique; however, a likely byproduct of regular mindfulness practice is that students will be less reactive and in more control of their impulses. This will certainly contribute to a classroom environment that is more conducive to learning and overall well-being.

Mindfulness and a More Compassionate World

Mindfulness is, first and foremost, a way to foster the development of the whole person. By giving students the opportunity to engage in daily mindfulness practices, we help them to be more present and aware. We strengthen their self-regulation skills; i.e., their ability to manage their own emotions, attention, and behavior. Mindfulness practice helps them become aware of their internal and external experiences, to notice when they are distracted, and to focus their attention where they want it to be and stay. It helps them respond wisely, rather than impulsively, and to be more compassionate and kind toward themselves and others. In many ways, this important work also helps to cultivate a more compassionate world.

I recently had the opportunity to hear Dr. Oliver Hill, Professor of Psychology at Virginia State University, speak about the impact and benefits of mindfulness. I was struck by his compelling argument that mindfulness can be seen as action toward social justice. When we have an underlying understanding and experience of mindfulness, it is expressed in how we live our lives. Mindfulness helps us be more aware of our interconnectedness and our judgments, biases, behaviors, and responses. With this awareness, we are more likely to transform how we interact with each other. It helps to change our perspectives and understanding so we can more mindfully and thoughtfully "serve the world." Dr. Hill suggests this positive and responsive way of operating in the world can contribute to an understanding of our interconnectedness and to positive social change. This idea resonates with me, as I think about our role as teachers in preparing children both for the world and to be good citizens in the world. It is daily practice worth investing in.

2

Getting Started

Whether you have just heard about mindfulness for the classroom and are interested in giving it a try or you are already on your way to creating a routine of teaching and practicing mindfulness with your students, there are key considerations, guiding principles, and introductory lessons to help set the stage for teaching, learning about, and practicing mindfulness in the classroom.

Key Considerations

Start with Your Own Practice

The most powerful mindfulness strategy in your classroom is your own practice. I remind people of a familiar safety message we receive on an airplane as we prepare for takeoff: the flight attendant reminds us to secure our own oxygen mask before helping others to secure theirs. We are advised to do this because if we were to run out of oxygen in an emergency, we would be helpless to support anyone else. This metaphor underscores the importance of self-care and the role it plays in preparing us to support and care for our students in the classroom. Mindfulness practice is one way to engage in self-care.

Research shows that, when teachers practice mindfulness, they are more likely to develop habits of mind that support stress reduction, emotion regulation, and overall physical and emotional well-being (Flook, 2015; Molloy et al., 2018; Murphy, 2017). This is especially important, as recent research found that teachers experience the highest rate of daily stress among all occupational groups, tied with nurses and higher than physicians (Greenberg, Brown & Abenavoli, 2016). Moreover, when teachers commit to a personal mindfulness practice, there is often a ripple effect in the classroom. Students are sensitive to your tone and demeanor and will respond to the presence you bring. According to neuroscientists, mirror

"Children have never been very good at listening to their elders, but they have never failed to imitate them."
— James Baldwin

Read how Heather Farragher, a high-school classroom teacher, describes her personal mindfulness practice influencing her teaching experience on page 29.

If you are aware that one of your students has experienced trauma, it is best to touch base with a school social worker or psychologist, and to communicate with parents, to get an opinion about whether mindfulness is appropriate for that student.

Patricia Jennings, an internationally recognized leader in the field of social and emotional learning and mindfulness, has written an excellent book entitled, *The Trauma-Sensitive Classroom: Building Resilience with Compassionate Teaching*. I recommend it highly.

neurons are neurons that fire both when we engage in an action and when we observe someone engage in an action (Rizzolatti & Sinigaglia, 2008). For example, when a student is acting out in class or they are watching their classmate act out, their brain activity will look strikingly similar. Similarly, if students observe and experience you acting calmly, mindfully, thoughtfully, and with presence on a regular basis, their mirror neurons help them resonate with these behaviors and possibly make them more likely to mimic them.

Finally, and perhaps most importantly, your own practice will give you the embodied experience necessary to teach and lead mindfulness in a way that is authentic. Your own practice will help you be more attuned to your students and their experiences of growth and challenge along the way. If you do not already have a dedicated personal practice, I encourage you to explore developing one alongside your students. It can be as simple as taking a moment or two each day to focus on your breathing before the school day starts, in the midst of your busy day as a reset, or as a gift to yourself at the end of the day. The key is to practice every day, whether it's for one minute, 10 minutes, or more. You will surely feel it and so will your students.

Ensure Mindfulness Practice Is Secular

Within your school setting, it is crucial to ensure that mindfulness practices are presented in ways that are secular. This means it is important that you do not use language, tools, symbols, or gestures that are linked in any way to particular religious or spiritual traditions; i.e., do not use words like "the soul" or "spirit," hand gestures, religious props, etc. The purpose of mindfulness practice within the school setting is to teach students skill-building exercises to help support present awareness, well-being, and self-management of attention, emotions and behaviors. In this way your teaching will be consistent with current scientific understanding and inclusive for all.

Be Trauma-Sensitive

While mindfulness practice is an excellent tool for helping to protect against and counteract the stress resulting from trauma, it can be triggering in some instances. As trauma expert David Treleaven has suggested, mindfulness does not cause trauma, but it might uncover it. You will not always know if your students have experienced trauma in the past or are currently experiencing it. This is why it is best to use trauma-informed strategies with all of your students. Give your students choice in how (or if) they practice mindfulness. Become trained in recognizing trauma symptoms and understanding how to respond to them skilfully. Become familiar with resources available in your school for students who may need additional support.

If an activity unexpectedly triggers one of your students is into a stress response (pupils dilated, shallow breathing, agitated behavior, clenched body, tears, withdrawal, freezing, etc.), respond immediately with kindness and compassion. If possible, help students switch into a relaxation response by offering them a number of alternative choices for mindfulness practice; e.g., Hoberman sphere, Mind Jar, Mindful Coloring, etc. Giving students the choice and opportunity to focus their attention on something external to their bodies can help them self-regulate and gain a sense of control and agency.

Differentiate for Diverse Student Needs

As teachers know, when we teach through the principles and guidelines of Universal Design for Learning (UDL) and differentiated instruction, we offer students multiple and flexible ways to learn and demonstrate what they know. This promotes an inclusive environment for all students who come to our classrooms from a variety of backgrounds and with various needs, strengths, learning styles, preferences, and interests. It also helps us teach in a culturally responsive way. We are most responsive to our students' needs when we have a good understanding of them as unique learners and offer them options and choice. As you would differentiate for any other learning opportunity, you can plan for mindfulness activities with student needs in mind.

There are a variety of activities that appeal to various learning styles, whether a student is a visual, auditory, tactile, or kinesthetic learner. Here are just a few considerations for planning in a way that is equitable and inclusive:

- For students with sound sensitivities, it is helpful to touch base with them about their level of comfort with the sound of a ringing bell, which is often used to signal the end a mindfulness practice. In the past, I have found if I simply ring the bell at the farthest point from a student who has sensitivities, it is often enough to keep them comfortable.
- For many students, incorporating visuals or concrete materials supports their focus and their understanding about what is expected during a particular mindfulness practice (see end of chapters for various visual supports).
- Invite students who are easily distracted to practice mindfulness in a part of the room that is typically quieter; e.g., away from a ticking clock, a doorway, fish tank, etc.
- Students who have a difficult time sitting still can be invited to stand or even move around (quietly) during certain mindfulness practices.
- As students learn various mindfulness activities, it may become clear that some students gravitate more toward certain activities than others. In this case, you might decide to offer them a choice of which mindfulness activity to engage in.

For the most part, as all mindfulness practices are designed to help students bring awareness to the present moment, the type of practice they engage in becomes somewhat incidental. You know your students best. How you bring mindfulness to them needs to reflect your needs and theirs.

Have Reasonable Expectations

Mindfulness practice may be new to many of your students. As we know, when we introduce anything novel to our class, there are a variety of initial responses. The majority of your students will take to the practices immediately, finding the peaceful and calming practices to be an experience they crave. You may notice that some students appear to daydream or even fall asleep in the midst of practices at first. Other students may initially resist, complaining or laughing or even acting out. Resistance is often a sign they are simply not used to intentional moments of calm in which they are asked to stop "doing" and just be.

For our students, who are steeped in a culture of distraction, mindfulness might feel somewhat uncomfortable or even threatening at first. For example, students with characteristics of inattention or hyperactivity can have a challenging time when asked to sit still and quiet for a period of time. This may result in some disruptive behavior. Hearken back to what Ross Greene said about challenging behaviors and their connection to unsolved problems or lagging skills to understand that a student could be acting out of fear, growing pains, or uncertainty, rather than disrespect. We must start where they are, cultivating an attitude of patience and compassion toward how they come to their experience of mindfulness.

It is important to be consistent in offering daily mindfulness practices to your students. Each moment of mindfulness practice makes the next moment of practice that much easier. So do not expect full participation or silence in the room in a class that is just learning mindfulness. As with any other type of learning, think of it as a process. Mindfulness is a life skill that must be cultivated and developed over time. There might be initial challenges (though often they are minimal); remember that they are part of the process and, ultimately, the growth. Students who initially resist mindfulness practice are often the students who need it the most, and will often end up committing wholeheartedly to daily practices. All that is needed was a growth mindset and a little bit of time.

Treat This Time Differently

While there are many documented benefits of mindfulness practice, it is a somewhat unique school activity in that there is no required outcome. The goal is for students to practice being in the present moment, for them to get out of their heads and into the here and now. This is in contrast to the rest of the school day, when our sights are set on desired learning goals and outcomes for our students. Mindfulness activities are best introduced in a way that sends a message to students that this time is carved out especially for them to engage in self-care.

It can be helpful to make slight changes to the environment to help distinguish this time from the rest of the school day. You might ask students to clear their desks or face their chairs in a different direction. Some teachers dim or turn off the lights, play calming music in the background, or chime a bell reserved for mindfulness practice. This signals a transition from worktime to mindfulness time. Some teachers have flexible seating in their classrooms, where students are invited to sit or lie wherever they are most comfortable (chairs, carpet, floor). Incorporating small but distinguishable changes to the environment helps students transition into a mindfulness-ready frame of mind.

Carol Dweck writes about *growth mindset* **and the importance of a child's belief in their ability to improve and learn. When students commit to practicing and sticking to something, especially in the face of challenge, this is considered a growth mindset. Teachers with a growth mindset recognize and cultivate opportunities for growth by offering repeated opportunities for their students to develop a skill.**

Do not Use Mindfulness as a Punitive Tool

I was invited into a fifth-grade classroom by a teacher who had recently initiated mindfulness practices in the classroom. As I came through the door, the teacher was attempting to redirect the off-task behavior of a good portion of the class. It was clear there was a need to reset the climate of the classroom. Suddenly, I heard the sound of the mindfulness bell. With a stern voice the teacher said, "This class has gotten out of control and I think it's time for a mindful moment to help you calm yourselves down." A few students responded with groans and eye rolls. My heart sank. Mindfulness should be offered to students as a welcome opportunity to practice self-care and to be peaceful, present, and still. Students will not experience mindfulness in this positive way when it is imposed as a consequence or as an obvious response to negative behavior. It will not take long for them to make a negative association.

It is important that mindfulness activities or mindful classroom spaces are not used as punitive tools or as consequences. How students experience mindfulness will be greatly influenced by the spirit in which it is offered to them. Timing matters, as does your tone. When behaviors begin to escalate or when students become somewhat disengaged, it would be helpful to take a break and have a mindfulness moment. It is all in how you frame it. The advice I gave to the fifth-grade teacher for next time was to use a neutral tone to say something like: "Why don't we take a break. I can see that many students have gotten off-task. It may be helpful to do a mindfulness practice to help you return to your work with more presence and attention." When mindfulness practice is framed and introduced as a positive and skill-building opportunity, students are much more likely to experience it as helpful and supportive. In fact, it is very common for students to recognize for themselves when their class is in need of a calming break and to ask for a mindful moment for all. This is the ultimate buy-in.

Give Mindfulness Invitation Status

Ultimately, the decision of whether or not to participate in mindfulness practice needs to be in the hands of your students. The very nature of mindfulness practice makes it impossible to compel students to engage. If they choose not to participate, it is important that they are given clear boundaries and expectations for what to do instead. I have invited students to sit quietly for a few moments, or to read or draw. Some students choose to put their heads down or look out the window. The only rule is they should not do anything to distract or disturb others who have made the choice to practice mindfulness.

Students should also be invited to close their eyes during mindfulness practice. Again, the choice of whether to close their eyes or, alternatively, to lower their head and look down, should be theirs. There are several reasons why students may not feel comfortable closing their eyes. Students who have experienced trauma, who have trust issues, or who simply feel uncomfortable might not want to lose sight of their surroundings. Over time, many students who start out with their eyes open come to close them during practice.

Preparing for Mindfulness

The "So What?"

I have observed students as young as five years old understand and articulate the benefits of mindfulness practice. I am reminded of a story told to me by two former teacher candidates, Caitlin and Elizabeth, who had just returned from team-teaching in their practicum placement in a Kindergarten classroom. They had been teaching their students about mindfulness and self-regulation. They used a tool called the breathing sphere to talk about using the breath to calm nervous systems and activate the wiser, thinking part of the brain. After engaging in this lesson one day, the bell rang and students left for recess. On their return, two students who were clearly in the midst of a conflict rushed into class. Students had been learning about conflict resolution and, as a result, were quickly directed to an area of the room reserved for conflict management. As Caitlin and

Elizabeth watched the attempt at conflict resolution unfold, they observed one of the students pick up the breathing sphere and gently begin to open and close it. The students sat in silence for 30 seconds and then began to talk. Afterward, when asked what they had been doing with the breathing sphere, one of the students raised their hand, pointed towards the word *self-regulation* on the board and said, "We were doing that!" In their own words, they went on to explain they knew they could better manage their emotions and their conflict if they started with mindful breathing to help them calm down so they could think more wisely and make better choices. This, from five year-olds after one brief lesson! This not only speaks to what is possible when students learn to practice mindfulness, it also underscores the importance of teaching students about what's in it for them.

When we take the time to explain why what we are teaching is meaningful, students are more likely to be intrinsically motivated to engage in what they are learning. Students who have an understanding of how and why mindfulness supports them are more likely to "opt in." Be sure to spend some time explaining the benefits of mindfulness and how various parts of the brain can be strengthened to support regulation of behaviors, thinking, learning, emotions, and overall well-being.

See Chapter 5 for a detailed lesson for how to explain the brain and the benefits of mindfulness.

The Ready Position

Let students know mindfulness is a time when bodies and minds are as still and quiet as possible. The expectation is that students will have "mindful bodies." Someone with a mindful body is quiet, as still as possible, and sitting up straight (no slouching) with arms and hands on laps or at sides. This is a ready position for mindfulness practice. It also means students are being respectful of others' space and are keeping movement to a minimum. I like to give students an opportunity to practice going back and forth between sitting with a mindful body and sitting without a mindful body (e.g., slouched, arms everywhere, head on the desk, legs stretched out wide, etc.). Giving them an opportunity to contrast these two ways of being in their bodies solidifies their understanding of what it means to be in a mindful body and ready for mindfulness practice.

While practicing mindfulness, students may be in close proximity to each other. This is especially true if they are engaging in a mindfulness practice while lying on a carpet. It is helpful to have a conversation about what it means to respect someone else's personal space. I engage students in an activity that helps them learn about the boundaries of their own personal space and to recognize and honor the personal space of others.

My Space Bubble: the Comfort Zone

Students are invited to stand far across from a partner. One at a time, one student takes slow steps towards the other. Their partner is prompted to hold their hand up like a stop sign to let the walking student know when they are "close enough"; anything beyond the stop sign would make the student feel uncomfortable. Students then switch places.

Daily Practice

When mindfulness is introduced as a routine and is consistent, it has the most positive effect on students. Research conducted by Dr. James E. Stahl and his team of Harvard researchers found that to experience the benefits of mindfulness practice we do not need to enrol in a formal program or spend hours each day practicing. What is most important is consistency. It is much better to practice for just a few minutes every day than to practice for an hour or more a few days a week. The positive impact of mindfulness is born out of daily routine. Even short but regular practices (a minute or two of mindful listening or mindful breathing) help chart new pathways in the brain that support our students in myriad ways.

Planning and Scheduling Mindfulness

Students respond most positively to their learning in the classroom when they are consulted about the process. Once students have been introduced to mindfulness and have participated in daily practices for a few weeks, it is very helpful to invite them to co-construct how mindfulness will be integrated into their school day. While it is helpful, for consistency and routine, to have a set time for a mindfulness practice each day, students can be consulted about which part(s) of the day they feel it would be best for them. Students often suggest having mindfulness practice either during or after a transition and, certainly, before and after testing.

Of course, every class and every group of students is different. Many teachers I know like to begin and end the day with a moment of mindful breathing. It helps set the tone for the start of the school day and for the transition home at the end of the day. Students may choose to include another brief practice during the day, either scheduled or impromptu. Once a routine is established, a rotating schedule can be created by which students are responsible for initiating a mindfulness practice with the sound of a bell. I promise you, they will remember their scheduled practice if you (or your substitute) ever forget!

Opportunities to Debrief

Give students opportunities to share the details of their experiences. Initially, most students are surprised and even frustrated by the fact that they have a seemingly endless stream of thoughts entering their minds as they engage in mindfulness practice. A typical comment from students is, "I'm bad at mindfulness because my mind keeps getting distracted." It is important to give them the chance to share their experiences of a wandering mind and to normalize it as part of the practice. They need to know that the rest of the class is experiencing the same thing. Provide time for a discussion about the nature of the mind, the importance of not being judgmental about their thoughts, and the imperative of simply noticing their thoughts and then returning back to their practice over and over again.

Giving students a chance to debrief also gives them an opportunity to hear from other students about how mindfulness practice helps them to be more present and in better control of their behaviors, attention, and emotions. It also gives them the chance to hear from other students who may not initially have a positive experience. Medical doctor and mindfulness educator Amy Saltzman suggests being upfront about what you expect students who resist might be thinking. She suggests prompting students ahead of their first practice to notice if they have thoughts about mindfulness practice being "dumb" or "a waste of time." This helps validate their thinking as okay, perhaps even expected. It gives them space to come to mindfulness practice in their own time.

Students can be given the opportunity to respond to their experiences in writing. This helps promote reflection and facilitate thoughtful and critical response, and provides a private outlet for their feelings and experiences. It also helps to consolidate learning and understanding. You will find many writing response activity sheet templates at the ends of chapters.

Communication with Parents

See page 30 for a reproducible letter to parents about mindfulness practice in the classroom.

It is a good idea to communicate with parents about your intention to include secular mindfulness practices within their child's daily classroom schedule. It is likely they have heard or read about mindfulness practices. They may have preconceived notions or incorrect understandings about how and why it is implemented in the school setting. Share your reasons for introducing mindfulness strategies and be prepared to back them up with research. Parents and guardians might have ongoing questions and it is important to share information and begin the conversation from the outset.

Elementary teacher Dana Chapman sends this philosophy statement to parents and caregivers at the start of the school year.

Voice from the Classroom: Sample Philosophy Statement
by Dana Chapman

Dear Families,

At the beginning of each school year, I like to take some time to offer my evolving philosophy of education to the families with whom I'll be spending the coming months. This year, I am thrilled to be writing as a new member of the XXX community—a place I already feel inspired by. The opportunity to work with colleagues, parents, and children who also share a belief in young people's ability to explore, investigate, and build knowledge is a gift. I have always enjoyed a wonderful relationship with the families of my students and I look forward to getting to know all of you. Please know that I will endeavor to meet the needs of your child both as a unique individual and as a contributing member of our classroom community. I look forward to these initial days of school where we will begin the process of getting to know one another and building our community.

Creating a calm, cooperative energy in a classroom does not happen by accident. I've realized that when an environment has been consciously established to support learning, there is no limit to where children can go. Two important pieces to this end are the creation of routines and a democratic attitude in which decisions are made as a group and challenges are tackled from a place of kindness and maturity. Another piece of the puzzle is cultivating ways of being in the room and fostering qualities such as mutual respect, attentive listening, participation, and giving and receiving compliments. Through various daily cooperative learning activities, the children learn to respect themselves, their classmates, and their environment; they gain skills as effective listeners; they see value in actively participating; and they learn to give "appreciations" to one another. The goals of these efforts are to build resiliency in children and to consciously move a group through the stages of community building. These stages are inclusion (getting to know one another), influence (embracing one another's gifts and quirks), and ultimately community (becoming a high-functioning group that can support one another and make decisions with ease).

Mindfulness practices are another invaluable component of a high-functioning learning environment. By mindfulness practices I mean things like relaxation and breathing techniques, yoga poses, and visualizations. This is an exciting area in education right now, perhaps in response to the fast-paced, highly stimulated environment children are immersed in. There is a tremendous amount of research being generated on the impact of mindfulness practices on children's social, emotional, and academic development. Incorporating movement, energizers, and mindfulness practices allows us to refocus, increase the learning potential, and maximize our time together. I've also been told many stories of these sorts of activities planting seeds for moments outside of school where tensions rise and children are able to calm down and recognize in themselves an ability to be still and strong.

I would argue the most important consideration in classroom management is the conscious establishment of a poetic heartbeat underlying everything that happens in the room, from the aesthetics and the quiet signals to the community circle discussions. This simply means that we take the time to notice. We notice the natural environment, we notice the incredible choice of words an author uses, and we notice the patterns all around us. Children will go to deep places if they feel safe and if they come to trust that observing, wondering, and questioning are honored. It is from these deep places that exciting learning can happen.

I believe when we step back and look at the big picture of what education should be, we must acknowledge the importance of literacy and numeracy skills, the necessity of strong problem-solving abilities and interpersonal skills, and the need for critical analysis and contemplation. When we focus on these skills in the classroom, we ultimately prepare our students to have a global impact in the future.

I look forward to spending an inspiring and magical year with you and your child!

Sincerely,
Dana Chapman

Resources and Tools

The only resource you really need to introduce mindfulness practices in your classroom is your students. Their presence and their breath is enough to begin. However, here is a list of resources and tools that may be used in correspondence with some of the activities outlined in this book:

Some of these items can be purchased; others are included as templates or instructions.

- Resonating chime/bell
- Mind Jar (see page 140)
- Objects that make sounds
- Anchor charts (see chapters for examples)
- Breathing sphere
- Coloring utensils
- Fidget tools
- Themed Read-alouds (see Professional Resources on page 157)
- Mindful Coloring (see page 142)
- Senses Cards (See pages 70–72)
- Yoga Pose Cards (See pages 117–120)
- Student worksheets to consolidate learning (see end of each chapter)
- Gratitude Cards, Tree, Leaves, and Journal (See Mindfulness of Emotions chapter for templates)
- Peace Corner (see Peace Corner chapter for details)
- Worry Box (see Mindfulness of Emotions chapter)

Introducing Mindfulness to Students

It is best to start small when first introducing mindfulness practices. Begin with a brief explanation of what mindfulness is and follow with a quick and simple exercise that is just one or two minutes long. As students feel more comfortable and begin to develop their skills, continue to increase the amount of time by just a few minutes over several weeks, according to your student's capacity to be in stillness and silence. Your students' level of presence and engagement will let you know when they are ready for more.

I begin by explaining what mindfulness is and then immerse students in a brief mindfulness practice from the outset. It gives them an opportunity for an embodied practice and it serves as a starting point for questions and discussion. Depending on the age and grade level, I then follow up with a lesson on defining the present moment and what it means to use an anchor for practice. Later, I teach about the benefits of mindfulness (see Chapter 8). Once students have been introduced to mindfulness through a few starter lessons, they are ready to engage in the individual mindfulness activities and practices found in the remaining chapters.

Starter Lesson: Mindful Listening with a Chime

This starter lesson uses Mindful Listening as an entry point for introducing mindfulness practice to your students. It begins with a definition of mindfulness. Then students listen to the sound of the chime as an object of focus (or *anchor*) to help root or ground them in the present moment. They are asked to listen mindfully and carefully to the resonating sound and to raise their hands when they can no longer hear it. Over just a few tries, their focus seems to sharpen and they can often hear the sound resonate for longer periods. They also learn to tap into what it feels like to be presently aware. For many of our students, this is a novel experience.

1. Have a chime or sound of a resonating bell ready (there are several available online for free).
2. Write the term *Mindfulness* on the interactive whiteboard, chart paper, or board.
3. Invite students into the practice:

   *We are going to practice something called mindfulness. Mindfulness is when you notice what is happening **right now**. When you are learning about and practicing mindfulness, it gives you a chance to act like a scientist by paying very careful attention to things, like what you are thinking and feeling, how your body feels, what you see or smell or taste, or what you notice is happening around you right now. When you are observing these things like a scientist, you are paying attention on purpose and practicing being in the **present moment**.*

4. Write the definition of mindfulness on the board for students to see:

   Mindfulness is paying very careful attention, like a scientist, to what you are thinking and feeling, how your body feels, what you see, hear, smell or taste, or what you notice is happening around you in the present moment.

I have used the following introductory starter lessons with students from 5 to 55 years old. The learning is the same.

It is helpful to have a bell or chime that has a resonating sound that lasts 10 seconds or longer. Alternatively, there are several free mindfulness bell apps available.

Use scripts as a guide. You may read as-is or modify to fit your needs.

5. Continue lesson:

So, today you are going to practice acting like a scientist while you practice something called mindful listening with the sound of a bell. You will be using your sense of hearing. Start by letting your body be still and comfortable in your chair. If you need to, rock left and right until you find the right spot. Sit up nice and straight with a mindful body and let your shoulders drop. Imagine there's a string at the top of your head and it's pulling your back up just a little straighter. Both of your feet should be touching the ground and your hands should be on your lap.

Close your eyes or let your chin drop a little and look down. When I ring the bell, try to listen very carefully and mindfully for as long as you can to the sound of the ringing. If your mind wanders, just bring your attention back to the sound of the bell. Keep your eyes closed or continue to look down. Raise your hand when you can no longer hear even a little bit of the sound of the bell.

6. Pause and ring the bell.
7. Once the sound of the bell recedes and all hands are raised, ask students to keep their eyes closed (or their chins dropped) and let them know you will be ringing the bell for them to listen to again.
8. Ring the bell for a second time.
9. Follow up with a short debrief and discussion. I typically ask students questions like *What was it like for you to be quiet and still while listening to just one sound? Did you get distracted? What happened when you heard other sounds? What did your body feel like when you were sitting still and listening? What did your mind feel like when you were sitting quiet and still? How was this experience of mindful listening different from how you usually listen? How did you feel afterward?* Students usually report their bodies feel relaxed and their minds feel calm.
10. It is very likely that at least one student will report being distracted at one point or another. This gives you an opportunity to talk about mindfulness and the nature of the mind:

Thank you for sharing that you were distracted a little bit during this mindful listening practice. Everyone gets distracted at one time or another when they are practicing mindfulness. This is what our minds do. Was anyone else distracted?
(Pause for responses)
We all have thoughts and feelings, and they come and go all the time. Even when you are trying very hard to pay attention and be in the present during mindfulness practice, your mind will wander a little bit, and that's okay. It's completely expected. In fact, it's part of the mindfulness practice. Did anyone get distracted but then notice that and bring their attention back to listening to the bell again?
(Pause for responses)
That's great, because that's what mindfulness practice is. It's about noticing when your mind wanders and gets distracted and then bringing your attention back to the present by focusing on the sound of the bell. Even if you do that over and over again, that's what mindfulness practice is. That's how our brains get stronger. Let's try the mindful listening exercise one more time.

11. Ask students to close their eyes (or let their chins drop) in preparation for mindful listening of the bell once again.
12. Ring the bell and take students through one more cycle of mindful listening with the chime exercise.

Starter Lesson: Defining the Present Moment

This follow-up lesson is optional.

Perhaps the most challenging concept for students to grasp is the notion of the **present** moment. Take a few minutes to have students define and understand what this means. One way to demystify the present is by differentiating it from both the past and the future.

1. On the interactive whiteboard, the blackboard, or piece of chart paper, create three columns with the headings *PAST, PRESENT, FUTURE*.

2. Explain to students that you will be working together to come up with examples related to the past, the present, and the future.

3. If necessary, begin by drawing from prior knowledge their understanding of the concepts of the past, the present, and the future (*the past is something that happened before now; the present is something happening now; the future is something that happens after now*).

4. Point to the word *PAST* in the first column. Ask students to think about and share something that happened in the past. Possible prompt questions: *What happened at recess? What happened this morning at home? What happened yesterday?* Record their responses.

5. Skip to the third column and point to the word *FUTURE*. Ask students to think about and share something that might happen in the future. Possible prompt questions: *What might you do when you are at home tonight? What might you eat for breakfast tomorrow? What might you do on the weekend?* Record their responses.

See Chapter 4 for more on Mindful Sensing.

6. Now move to the middle column labelled *PRESENT*. Ask students to use their senses, like a scientist, to notice what is happening right now. Possible prompt questions: *What do you see? What do you hear? What do you smell?* Record their responses.

7. After completing the chart together, invite students to share their understanding of the difference between the past and the future.

8. Ask students what it means to notice something in the present. Potential responses: *something happening right now; something we can notice with our senses right now; something we are paying attention to in this moment.*

9. Return to the definition of mindfulness: *Mindfulness is paying very careful attention to what you are thinking and feeling, how your body feels, what you see, or hear or smell or taste, or what you notice is happening around you in the **present** moment.*

10. To help consolidate learning, invite students to work independently or in pairs to complete the Tapping into the Present Moment through Your Senses activity sheet (see page 31). Students are given an opportunity to practice noticing what they are experiencing with each of their five senses "right now."

Voice from the Classroom: Mindfulness for Teachers
by Heather Farragher

I am a high-school English teacher and librarian. I start each of my classes by giving students the opportunity to practice mindfulness, write gratitude lists, color or draw, try out new mindfulness apps, or listen to a body scan. Despite feeling the benefits of mindfulness in the classroom, it took me some time to commit to a daily personal practice. In the busyness of my life, it felt as though I had no time. Still, the idea of committing to my own practice was always percolating in my mind.

Last September, I began a new school year in a new position. I decided to listen to the inner voice telling me that, despite all of the things I couldn't control, I could choose how I began each day. At first, my daily practice consisted of lying on my yoga mat each morning for a minimum of ten minutes to listen to a guided meditation and do yoga. Let's be real, I fell asleep more than a few times. It took a few days to adjust to this routine but before I knew it I was easily spending half an hour practicing. I thought the hardest part would be practicing before doing anything else in the morning because I practically wrote my to-do list in my sleep and woke up already feeling behind. Fortunately, by the second week, practicing in the morning became a natural and enjoyable transition into my day.

I no longer buy into the idea that there isn't enough time in the day for mindfulness or self-care. After a few minutes of deep breathing and focusing on the present moment, I feel more grounded, content, and ready to greet what is ahead of me in the day. As a result of that, I've become more patient and understanding in my classroom (though I still have my moments). I now know that a few deep breaths can powerfully alter how I respond to my students and to the challenges of the day.

I now recognize when I am feeling overwhelmed and stretched too thin. With this awareness, I am now much more likely to take a break during the day, ask for help if I need it, sleep more, and work out or engage in other self-care activities. This makes it less likely that I carry my stress into my classroom and it allows me to show up for my students in ways they need and deserve. The calmness and connection that it has brought to my life has also permeated my classroom. As a result, I enjoy the time I spend with each of my students more, listen to them more, laugh more, and see my students more clearly for who they are. The majority of my students appreciate the time we spend being mindful and find it to be just as relaxing, calming, and comforting as I do. Like me, they crave time to be still and present during their busy lives.

Since committing to a regular practice, I've enjoyed work more and can truly see myself in this caring profession for the long-term. These benefits greatly outweigh the struggle it was to get started and stay committed to a regular practice. Going forward, I know I will continue with a daily mindfulness practice of some sort and, though it may not always look the same, I'll always have time for even just three deep breaths. Sometimes that's all it takes.

Introductory Letter to Parents

Dear Parent/Guardian(s),

I'm excited to share details with you about some of the techniques and strategies being used in our classroom to help support your child's well-being and learning. Part of my promise to my students and to you is to create learning conditions that help your child feel calm, focused, and ready to learn. One very important skill set we are working on is self-regulation. Self-regulation refers to your child's ability to manage their attention, behaviors, and emotions. This set of skills has been shown to be more important than IQ when it comes to predicting a child's ability to do well in school. One of the techniques we have begun to integrate into our day to help teach and strengthen self-regulation is mindfulness practice. Mindfulness is a state of mind that encourages greater awareness of what is happening in the moment. It is a critical life skill. Mindfulness activities are a secular and research-based way to support and strengthen this habit of mind.

Scientific studies have shown regular mindfulness practice helps to improve resilience and academic performance. By beginning and ending each school day with a 2- to 5-minute mindfulness activity, such as focusing on the breath or engaging in mindful movement, your child is improving their ability to

- Focus their attention
- Reduce stress and anxiety
- Ignore distractions and stay on task
- Manage their behaviors and emotions
- Reflect on their thinking
- Formulate a goal and plan actions
- Be more empathetic and compassionate citizens
- Be more present

I have no doubt that your child will be excited to share their experiences with you. Please do not hesitate to contact me if you have any questions.

Pembroke Publishers ©2019 *Fostering Mindfulness* by Shelley Murphy ISBN 978-1-55138-340-8

Tapping into the Present Moment through Your Senses

The present is what is happening right now. Take a few minutes to notice what you are experiencing through each of your senses right now. If you don't notice anything through one or more of your senses, that's okay. Just notice that.

sight

With my eyes, right now I see:

hearing

With my ears, right now I hear:

smell

With my nose, right now I smell:

taste

With my mouth, right now I taste:

touch

With my body, right now I feel:

Pembroke Publishers ©2019 *Fostering Mindfulness* by Shelley Murphy ISBN 978-1-55138-340-8

3

Mindful Breathing

"I took a deep breath and listened to the old brag of my heart."
— Sylvia Plath, *The Bell Jar*

What Is Mindful Breathing?

We breathe to live. In fact, we typically breathe 960 breaths an hour and more than 23,000 breaths a day. Our miraculous brain stems automatically take care of these breaths for us by regulating their depth and rate depending on what our bodies need. None of this requires our attention. In contrast, *mindful breathing* is an exercise in purposefully paying attention to our breathing, using our breath as a focus for concentration to help keep us in the present moment. We do this by focusing on the inhalation and exhalation of our breath as we allow thoughts, emotions, and sensations to come and go in the background. When we focus on the breath, we notice our minds tend to jump from one thought to another. This is the nature of our minds. The goal of mindful breathing is to help us notice when our minds have been distracted and to repeatedly bring our attention back to our breathing. We may notice our breath in the rise and fall of our bellies or our chests, or the air coming in and out of our noses. Through mindful breathing, we are making a conscious choice to pay attention to our in-breath and out-breath. When the mind wanders (oh, and it will!), we just bring our attention back to our breath. This is mindful breathing.

Our students have a profound and powerful tool at their disposal. In fact, it is quite literally under their noses. It is their breath. Perhaps this is why mindful breathing is a core mindfulness practice. The physical sensation of the breath is always with us and can be used as an anchor to return to the present moment. Think of a boat that drops an anchor to remain in a stable position. While currents or waves may cause the boat to wander, the anchor keeps the boat secure, ensuring it does not drift away. In this same way, students can use their breath as an anchor point when their minds naturally wander off.

Research shows simple and regular mindful breathing exercises help strengthen children's control over their emotions, attention, self-regulation, and learning. This happens as a result of the repeated redirection of their minds back

It is important to note that it might not be comfortable for all students to focus on their breathing as an anchor for mindfulness practice. Students with respiratory challenges, asthma and emphysema, bronchitis or colds, etc. might experience feelings of anxiety when asked to pay careful attention to their breath. For these students, it is important to give them alternative options; e.g., mindful sensing, imagery, etc.

to their breath. It also happens as they develop a deeper connection to their breath and their breathing naturally becomes deeper, quieter, slower, and more regular. Quite naturally, their exhalation becomes longer than their inhalation, which sends a message to their brain to slow or calm their nervous system. This is important because the depth and rate of their breath has a profound impact on students' daily experience. When we are stressed, our fight-or-flight response is activated, our blood pressure rises, and our heart rate and breathing rate quicken. This makes it difficult to think clearly. The good news is that breath work is an excellent tool for interrupting the fight-or-flight response. We can actually use our breathing to talk our brain into helping us feel calm, which ultimately lowers blood pressure and heart rate and helps us think clearly.

When our breathing becomes deeper, slower, quieter, and more regular, the amygdala (the fight-or-flight centre of the brain) is calmed. The prefrontal cortex (the conscious thinking and reasoning part of the brain) is strengthened; this part of the brain is associated with higher-order brain functions such as awareness, concentration, and decision-making.

Tips for Teaching Mindful Breathing

- Mindful breathing exercises can be seamlessly, easily, and quickly integrated into the classroom schedule in just moments at any point during the day—at the beginning and end of the day, before or after a transition, before or after tests or exams.
- It is helpful to schedule 5 to 10 minutes throughout the day when students can expect a mindfulness practice. This way it becomes a natural part of their day.
- Students can sit, stand, or lie down for mindful breathing.
- If students are sitting at their desks, invite them to move their chairs away from their tables and turn them toward the area of the room where you are standing or sitting.
- Invite students to close their eyes or look down. Invite students to put one or both hands on their belly.
- You can begin and/or end mindful breathing exercises with the sound of a bell.
- Start with 30 seconds to one minute and increase the number of minutes as students become more comfortable and tolerant.
- Let students know ahead of time that their minds will wander—a lot—and that this is completely expected. Their realization that their mind has wandered and bringing it back to their breath over and over again is the mindfulness practice.
- For students who have difficulty sitting still, invite them to stand.

Many teachers use a vibratone or chime to begin and/or end mindful breathing. The bell should be different from any other tone you use to get the attention of your students.

Breath Activities

Before introducing formal mindful breathing practices to students, it is helpful to give students an opportunity to become aware of and learn about their breath. Awareness of breath is an integral part of each mindfulness practice. These introductory activities bring awareness to the breath, and involve play, movement, and visualization.

You can purchase a Hoberman sphere or invite students to use their hands to make their own breathing sphere.

Breathing Sphere Activities

A breathing sphere is an excellent visual tool for modelling how the lungs expand and contract as we inhale and exhale. As students observe the expanding and contracting of the breathing sphere, they follow along with their breath. They inhale as the sphere expands and exhale as the sphere contracts. As they watch the sphere and mimic its pace with their own breathing, they deepen their conscious awareness of their own breath.

Hoberman Sphere Breathing

Patented by Chuck Hoberman, a Hoberman sphere is an isokinetic structure that resembles a geodesic dome. It is capable of folding down to a fraction of its normal size by the scissor-like action of its joints (see image in margin). If you are using the commercially bought sphere, follow these steps to model how to use the sphere and then invite students to join in.

Hoberman Sphere, US © Charles Hoberman

1. Begin by making sure the breathing ball is contracted (not expanded).
2. Using both hands, gently hold the breathing ball in front of your belly. On opposite sides of the sphere's surface, hold one square.
3. Take a deep breath in as you slowly expand the sphere. Be sure to choose a pace that is not too slow for younger students.
4. Allow the sphere to slowly contract to its smallest size as you model breathing out.
5. Repeat one more time.
6. Invite students to join in for 5–7 breath cycles.
7. Ask students to Think–Pair–Share (think for a moment, then turn to a partner to share) what this experience was like for them. They may be asked to think about how this was different from how they normally breathe and/or how they are feeling after trying this activity.

Hand Sphere

While a commercial sphere might be convenient to use, it is not necessary. Students can create their own spheres with their hands. This gives them an opportunity to practice sphere breathing at home. Follow these steps to model how to create and use the handmade sphere and then invite students to join in.

1. Hold your palms and fingers together in front of your chest.
2. As you inhale deeply, separate your palms and expand your hands while keeping your fingertips and thumbs touching.
3. Slowly bring your palms back together as you model breathing out.
4. Repeat two more times.
5. Invite students to create their own spheres, starting with their hands and fingers together in front of their chests.
6. Before asking them to sync their sphere with their breathing, circulate the room to make sure they are able to expand their "sphere" properly; e.g., some students forget to keep their fingers touching.
7. Once all students have made their spheres properly, invite them to practice for 5–7 breath cycles. Students may try this individually or in partners.
8. Ask students to Think–Pair–Share (think for a moment, then turn to a partner to share) what this experience was like for them. They may be asked to think about how this was different from how they normally breathe; how they are feeling after trying this activity; etc.

Photo courtesy of Chris Urquhart

Voice from the Classroom: Alternative to Mindful Breathing
by Chris Urquhart

Breathwork is posited as the cornerstone of almost all mindfulness practices, reflecting the rich history of practices associated with breathwork across the globe. However, some students have a difficult time focusing on their breath due to challenges such as anxiety, emphysema, asthma, lung/chest trauma, or chronic bronchitis. It is therefore important to consider different entry points into mindfulness practice beyond focusing on the breath. The Hoberman Sphere is a popular teaching tool for mindfulness in the elementary classroom. It is often used to model the expanding and contracting of the lungs as we breathe. For students who prefer not to focus on their breath, you might considering using the sphere to invite students to focus on mindful seeing. Instruct students to view the colorful sphere carefully as it expands and contracts. They can be invited to focus on every detail they see. This gives all students an opportunity to use the very popular Hoberman Sphere as an entry point for mindfulness.

Pinwheels

A pinwheel is another excellent tool for helping students become familiar with the power of their breath. Students receive feedback from observing how quickly or slowly the pinwheel turns in reaction to their breath: quick or slow, deep or shallow, and loud or quiet. They also receive feedback from their minds and bodies as the depth and pace of the breath changes. When students are prompted to breathe deeply and slowly, it gives them an opportunity to activate their parasympathetic nervous system, which has a calming effect. As students become aware of this, it helps them learn they have tools at their disposal to help calm down the nervous system when they are angry or upset. Their breath is one of the most powerful tools they have. The pinwheel helps them understand this.

1. Depending on how many pinwheels you have, invite one, a few, or all students to hold their pinwheels with the sideways edge facing them.
2. Begin by inviting students to take a long, deep, slow breath in.
3. Next, invite students to blow on their pinwheel with a long, slow, loud exhalation. Prompt students to bring their awareness to their breath as they do this.
4. Repeat two or three times. Prompt students to notice how the pinwheel is turning and how their bodies and minds feel.
5. Next, invite students to blow on their pinwheels using quick, shallow breaths. Prompt students to bring their awareness to their breath as they do this.
6. Repeat two or three times. Prompt students to notice how the pinwheel is turning and how their bodies and minds feel.
7. Finally, invite students to blow on their pinwheel with a regular breath. Prompt students to bring awareness to their breath as they do this.
8. Repeat two or three times. Prompt students to notice how the pinwheel is turning and how their bodies and minds feel.
9. To conclude, have a whole-group or Think–Pair–Share discussion about whether they noticed a difference in how their minds and bodies felt when they were breathing quickly from when they were breathing slowly. Ask

them what they learned about their breathing. You may want to write these prompt questions on the board for students who would benefit from both hearing and reading the prompts.

Birthday Candle Activity

Use scripts as a guide. You may read as-is or modify to fit your needs.

Most students will have observed or experienced candles on a birthday cake being blown out. If the ritual is familiar to them, this activity helps to harness that memory to help them become aware of their breathing. Once the Birthday Candle Activity has been introduced to students, they can be prompted at any point throughout the day to "take a deep breath in and blow out the birthday candles" when they are feeling anxious, agitated, or angry.

1. Ask students to sit down, close their eyes, or look down in front of them.
2. Invite students into the practice:

   Imagine a birthday cake with lots of lit candles on it. Take a nice deep breath in through your nose and imagine you are blowing the candles out with a forceful breath from your mouth.
   (Pause)
   But wait. These are the kind of candles that blow out and then light up again. Take another deep breath in through your nose and blow the candles out again.

3. Repeat the script one or two more times.
4. Prompt students to Think–Pair–Share what they noticed about their breath and how their bodies and minds felt after blowing the candles out several times.

Introducing Guided Mindful Breathing

The mindful breathing scripts can be modified depending on age and grade level.

Once students have become familiar with and accustomed to noticing their breath, the following exercises introduce students to formal mindful breathing practice. It is best to begin by practicing for just a couple of minutes to start. Increase the amount of time as students become more comfortable and familiar with the practice. Students can be invited to put one or both hands on their belly to help them notice the rise and fall as they breathe in and breathe out; this often helps them stay focused on their breathing.

Three Deep Breaths

When first introducing this exercise for your students, you may find it helpful to model what a mindful deep breath looks and sounds like.

This introductory breathing exercise gives students an opportunity to learn how to use the pace and pattern of their breathing to calm down their nervous systems as they take just three deep breaths. It takes less than a minute and gives students a tool they can use wherever and whenever they are feeling stressed. This exercise also lays the foundation for many of the remaining exercises and lessons throughout the book.

1. Invite students into the practice:

   Today you are going to learn about and practice something called Three Deep Breaths. The exciting thing about this exercise is that once you learn it, you can use your Three Deep Breaths wherever you are to help you feel less stressed and more at peace. The more you practice, the more it will help you.

Let's start. Without forcing it, take a nice, deep breath in through your nose. You should feel your belly rising as you inhale. Now breathe out slowly and smoothly through your mouth. Do this two more times.

2. You can invite students to share how their bodies and minds feel after trying Three Deep Breaths. Invite them to share examples of scenarios when they could use Three Deep Breaths to help them calm down.

Mindful Breathing

This introductory mindful breathing exercise guides students to focus on their breath and to return to it when their minds wander.

1. Invite students into the practice:

   Let your bodies get comfortable in your chair. If you need to, rock left and right until you find just the right spot. Sit up with your back straight and let your shoulders drop. Imagine there's a string at the top of your head and it's pulling your back up just a little straighter. Both feet are touching the ground and your hands are on your belly. You can close your eyes or let your chin drop a little and look down.

   We are going to start by taking three nice deep breaths. At your own pace, breathe in through your nose and breathe out through your mouth. You'll do this three times.
   (Pause)
   Now go back to breathing as you usually do and keep your attention on your breath. Let your breath find its own rhythm.

   Notice your breath moving into your body and your breath moving out of your body. Notice your hands rising up as you breathe in and falling as you breathe out. It's like imagining your hands are riding the waves of your breathing.
   (Pause)
   Notice when your mind gets distracted and wanders away from noticing your breath. It's okay that your mind does this, because that's what minds do. You might start noticing your thoughts instead of your breath. Or you might notice sounds around you or feelings in your body. This is completely expected. Just notice when this happens and then bring your attention back to your breathing over and over again. When you do this, you are practicing mindfulness.

   Now I'm going to be silent for a few moments. Use this time to continue to notice your breathing until you hear the sound of the bell. After that, you can open your eyes.

2. After students have opened their eyes, invite them to Think–Pair–Share what the experience of mindful breathing was like for them.
3. You can invite students to complete the Writing Prompt after Mindful Breathing activity sheet on page 49 or 50. This activity sheet invites students to share details about how they felt before and after mindfulness, and to use pictures or words to describe what it was like to try mindful breathing.

Thoughts as Clouds

Most of us have spent some time watching clouds go by in the sky. It can be a very relaxing experience. In this exercise students are prompted to watch their thoughts go by, just as they would watch a cloud go by in the sky. The sky is a metaphor for students' minds. The clouds are a metaphor for thoughts and sensations that come and go.

Thoughts as Clouds teaches students about the nature of their minds and about letting their thoughts come and go as they focus on their breathing. Rather than trying to push their thoughts away or ignoring them, they are asked to simply notice them come and go without being drawn into them. This can be a very powerful lesson in teaching students that they are not their thoughts. They will learn, instead, that they are the observer of their thoughts.

1. Let students know this is an exercise that asks them to use their imaginations to picture a blue sky and some clouds moving in it.
2. Take a moment or two to draw on prior knowledge/experience of noticing clouds moving in the sky. If possible, show a brief video clip of a blue sky with moving clouds to prompt their imaginations for this exercise.
3. Invite students into the practice:

   Let your body get comfortable in your chair. If you need to, rock left and right until you find just the right spot. Sit up with your back straight and let your shoulders drop. Imagine there's a string at the top of your head and it's pulling your back up just a little straighter. Make sure that both feet are touching the ground and your hands are on your belly. You can close your eyes or let your chin drop a little and look down. When you're ready, turn your attention to your breathing. Notice your breath moving into your body and your breath moving out of your body.
   (Pause)
   Now, you are going to create a picture in your mind of a blue sky. Notice how blue it is.
   (Pause)
   Now you begin to notice there are some white puffy clouds moving across your sky.
   (Pause)
   Notice these clouds are beginning to cross from one side of your sky to the other. Don't try to force them across. Just notice them quickly moving into your sky and then disappearing from your sky. Notice them coming and going.
   (Pause)
   As you see your clouds come and go, you also notice that the blue part of your sky stays exactly the same.
   (Pause)
   It stays as blue as it was before.

   Now, imagine the sky is your mind and the clouds are your thoughts. Just like the clouds come and go in the sky, notice your thoughts and then let them go. When you are practicing mindfulness, you will have lots of thoughts, because that's what our minds do. Don't try to force them away. Just notice them like clouds moving through your sky.

   While you do that, I'm going to be silent for a minute or two. Use this time when I'm not saying anything to continue to notice your breathing. When thoughts come into your mind, just notice them and let them go. Notice and let go. Notice and let go. When you hear the sound of the bell and you're ready, you can open your eyes.

4. Invite students to Think–Pair–Share their experience of noticing thoughts as clouds.
5. You can invite students to complete the Thoughts are Like Passing Clouds activity sheet on page 48. This activity sheet invites students to record what thoughts came and went as they were trying this exercise. They are invited to draw or use words to consolidate learning.

Breath Counting

Counting the breaths during a mindfulness exercise adds structure to the practice and can be especially helpful for someone who has a very agitated or distracted mind. The counting acts as feedback and a reminder to keep awareness focused on the breath. Counting helps to give the mind a familiar and predictable pattern to help students focus and feel calm.

Counting Breath

This first activity simply asks students to focus on the count of their breath as they exhale.

1. Invite students into the practice:

   Let your body get comfortable in your chair and let your shoulders drop. Relax your jaw and let your mouth open just slightly. Imagine there is a string at the top of your head and it's pulling your back up a little straighter. Both feet are touching the ground and your hands are on your lap.

   To begin this exercise, count "One" to yourself as you exhale. The next time you exhale, count "Two," and so on up to "Five." Count only when you exhale and don't count higher than five. Be sure to notice that there is a slight pause at the end of your in-breath and another pause at the end of your out-breath. Continue to count each time you exhale. When you notice that you are no longer focusing on your counting, this means your mind has wandered. Just notice where your mind has wandered to and then bring your attention back to counting your breath until you hear the sound of the bell.

2. You can invite a whole-class or Think–Pair–Share discussion on how students experienced this exercise.

Thumb-Breath Counting

This activity invites students to use the touch of their thumb against each of their fingers to help anchor their mindful breath. It is helpful to demonstrate this for students before beginning. After each in-breath and out-breath, their thumb will move on to touch the next finger. Students are instructed to touch their thumb and their pointer finger after their first inhalation and exhalation (*1*); then to touch their thumb to their middle finger (*2*); then to touch their thumb to their ring finger (*3*); and to touch their thumb to their pinky finger (*4*). Each time they finish an in-and-out breath cycle, they move their thumb onto another finger. When they reach their final pinky finger, they start over again by touching their thumb and index finger after their inhalation and exhalation.

1. Model one round of Thumb-Breath Counting for your students.
2. Invite students into the practice:

   Let your body get comfortable in your chair and let your shoulders drop. Relax your jaw and let your mouth open just slightly. Imagine there is a string at the top of your head and it's pulling your back up just a little straighter. Both feet are touching the ground and your hands are on your lap. Turn your awareness to one of your hands.

   Start with this hand resting on your thigh with your palm up as you slowly inhale through your nose and exhale through your mouth. When you are ready, at the end of each in-breath and out-breath, you are going to touch your thumb to one of your fingers. Start by touching your thumb to your pointer finger after you inhale and exhale. Then move your thumb to your middle finger after you inhale and exhale again. Next is your fourth finger; and finally your pinky finger. Then you'll start all over again.

Just remember not to move your thumb until you have inhaled and exhaled once. Just stay with the feel of your fingers touching. When you notice that you are no longer focusing on your fingers touching, this means your mind has wandered. Just notice where your mind has wandered to and then bring your attention back to the feel of your fingers touching until you hear the sound of the bell.

3. You can invite a whole-class or Think–Pair–Share discussion on how students experienced this exercise.

Buddy Breathing

This breathing exercise helps children to focus on their breathing with the help of a favorite tiny object from home, a rock, or even an eraser. For older students, sitting in their chairs and with one or both hands on their bellies, one hand can become the anchor or object of focus. It can be especially effective if the "buddy" has some height, so the students can watch it rise and fall.

1. In preparation for this activity, ask younger students to bring in a favorite small toy or object. You could also use objects already in the classroom.
2. Invite students to come to the carpet with their object and lie down.
3. Be sure to instruct them to be mindful of others around them. There should be space between each student so that no one is touching.
4. Ask students to place their tiny object or a hand on their belly. If they are using a tiny object, their hands should be at their sides.
5. Walk around to ensure each object or hand is placed on their belly before you begin.
6. Continue the lesson:

   Lying down (or sitting) comfortably, place your favorite object (or hand) on your belly. Make sure it's in the middle so it doesn't fall off.
   (Pause)
   Now, turn your attention to your breathing.
   (Pause)
   Count to three on the in-breath and count to three on the out-breath. So breathe in—1, 2, 3—and breathe out—1, 2, 3. While you are breathing in and out, notice how your object (or hand) rises up when you inhale and goes down when you exhale.
   (Pause)
   Notice how the object stays still for a second or two after you breathe in and for a second or two after you breathe out. Now I'm going to be quiet for about 30 seconds. Continue to notice your buddy as it rises and falls on your belly until you hear the sound of the bell.

7. You can invite a whole-class or Think–Pair–Share discussion on how students experienced this exercise.

Kristen Lisowski's Kindergarten class did Buddy Breathing mindfulness practice using rocks they made themselves. Kristen helped students use air-dry clay and paint to personalize their rocks.

Snake Breathing and Bumblebee Breathing give students an opportunity to focus on their breath while increasing the length of time of their exhalation. When the length of their exhalation is a little longer than the length of their inhalation, students are able to activate their relaxation response. Students are often surprised at how long they can make the sounds with their out breath. At first, these exercises elicit lots of noise and, at times, laughter. For this reason, they're student favorites.

Snake Breathing

This is a quick and easy breathing exercise that many teachers like to invite students to do just before a test or exam, after an exam, or when students are agitated and need to reset.

1. Model a few cycles of this breathing for your students. In order to model, take a deep breath in through your nose and exhale through your teeth while you make a hissing sound. You should sound like a snake.
2. Invite students into the practice:

   Begin by taking a nice deep breath in through your nose. Now, exhale slowly through your teeth making a long, slow "hissing" sound like a snake—Ssssss.

3. Ask students to repeat three times.
4. You can invite a whole-class or Think–Pair–Share discussion on how students experienced this exercise.

Bumblebee Breathing

This breathing exercise, like the Snake Breathing exercise, gives students an opportunity to focus on their breath while increasing the length of time of their exhalation.

1. Model a few cycles of this breathing for your students. In order to model, take a deep breath in through your nose and exhale through your teeth while you make a buzzing sound. You should sound like a bumblebee.
2. Invite students into the practice:

   Begin by taking a nice deep breath in through your nose. Now, exhale slowly through your teeth while making a buzzing sound—Bzzzzz.

3. Ask students to repeat three times.
4. You can invite a whole-class or Think–Pair–Share discussion on how students experienced this exercise.

Elephant Breathing

This breathing exercise incorporates movement. Students can do this exercise while sitting down or standing up. Many prefer to stand for this activity, as they find it fun to role play being an elephant.

1. Model a few cycles of this breathing for your students: take a deep breath and raise hands with fingers interlocked over your head; hold for a few seconds and imagine spraying water out of your hands; breathe out, bringing your hands down.
2. Invite students into the practice:

   While sitting or standing, interlock your fingers and rest your hands on your lap. Take a nice, deep breath in and, at the same time, raise your hands up over your head/to the sky.
   (Pause)
   Stay like that for a few seconds and imagine you are spraying water out of your trunk.
   (Pause)
   When you breathe out, bring your hands back down.

3. Ask students to repeat three times.
4. You can invite a whole-class or Think–Pair–Share discussion on how students experienced this exercise.

Back-To-Back Partner Breathing

This breathing exercise gives students an opportunity to expand their awareness out of their own bodies and their own breath to their partner's breathing. Students enjoy the supportive aspect of this exercise and find they become more relaxed and calm because they are practicing with someone else. It also helps to foster an awareness of other, empathy, and a sense of community.

If there is a group of three, students can sit in the shape of a triangle with shoulders touching as they each face outward.

1. Get students into partners. If there is an odd number of students, have one group of three.
2. Invite students to sit comfortably on the floor, back-to-back with their partner. Students sit with a tall posture; legs can be crossed or in whatever position is most comfortable.
3. Walk around to ensure that students are sitting comfortably, back-to-back and ready to begin.
4. Invite students into the practice:

   You should all be back-to-back with your partner or partners and sitting as tall as possible. Imagine a string is coming from the bottom of your lower back all the way up through the top of your head. It's pulling you up just a little bit taller. Close your eyes or look down in front of you. Put your hands on your belly and notice the support you feel from your partner's back. Now turn your attention to your breathing. Notice your breath as you take three long, slow, deep breaths in and out.
   (Pause for three breaths)
   Return to your regular breathing and notice the rhythm of your breath as it comes into your body and as it moves out of your body.
   (Pause)

Now turn your attention to the rhythm of your partner's breathing. Just notice as they breathe in and out. Are they breathing faster than you? Slower than you? Where do you feel their breathing on your back? On your lower back? On your upper back?
(Pause)
See if you can match your partner's breathing with your own breathing. How does it feel to share the same rhythm of breath? Continue focusing on your partner's breathing.
(Pause for 15–30 seconds)
Now turn your attention back to your own breathing until you hear the sound of the bell.

5. Invite students to Think–Pair–Share their experience of back-to-back breathing.
6. You can invite students to complete the Back-to-Back Breathing activity sheet on page 51 or 52. This activity sheet invites students to use words or images to describe what they notice and how they felt during back-to-back mindful breathing to consolidate learning.

Square Breathing

It is best to begin by doing three rounds of Square Breathing and build from there.

This mindful breathing exercise (also sometimes called box breathing or four-part breathing) is a highly effective strategy that can be practiced by students for a minute or more to help them quickly calm their minds and bodies and prepare them for thinking, attending, and learning. It can be used on its own or as an entry point for the beginning of a mindful breathing practice.

- Check with students if they have breathing issues, as this exercise may not be appropriate for them.
- It's important to note that the count of four may be faster or slower for some.

Steps 1 and 2 are optional.

1. The first time you take students through this exercise, ask them to become aware of their normal breathing pattern. Give them 10 seconds or so just to notice the pace of their breath without manipulating it in any way.
2. Ask students to count how many seconds it takes for each inhalation and each exhalation. For example, they may notice that it takes two seconds for them to inhale and two seconds for them to exhale. Two seconds, then, is their starting point for progressively longer counts of breathing: inhale for a count of two, hold for a count of two, exhale for a count of two and hold, again, for a count of two. As they become comfortable with this count, they increase the length of their inhalation and exhalation by one second for a few rounds. Once they are used to this slower rate, they can increase their inhalation and exhalation by another second. If they are feeling uncomfortable or out of breath at all, it means they have slowed their breathing too quickly.

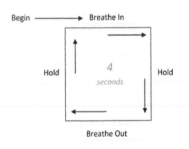

3. Draw a large square on the board, chart paper, whiteboard, or interactive whiteboard. Label it as in the diagram in the margin. Using your finger to follow around the square, model Square Breathing for your students: inhale for the count of four through your nose, hold for the count of four, exhale through your mouth for the count of four, and then hold again for another count of four. The in-breath, out-breath, and two pauses are meant to be the same length, just as each side of a square is the same length.

43

When guiding your students through Square Breathing for the first few times, you can support by counting the beats through for them; see counting in parentheses in script.

4. Once students understand the steps for Square Breathing, invite them to draw their square with their index finger in the air, on their desk, on the palm of their hand or their thigh. Younger students can be given a template for Square Breathing to trace.

5. You will likely need to read the script only for the first few times students try Square Breathing. Once they become familiar with the exercise, they will no longer need to be guided.

> *Begin by inhaling for a count of 4 (2, 3, 4).*
> *Hold for 4 (2, 3, 4).*
> *Exhale for 4 (2, 3, 4).*
> *Hold again for 4 (2, 3, 4).*

6. You can invite students to complete the Square Breathing activity sheet on page 53. This activity sheet provides a Square Breathing template with directions and a space for students to record their experiences.

4–7–8 Breathing

Many years ago, I attended a learning workshop presented by Andrew Weil, M.D. He was teaching about the power of the breath to promote health and well-being. One of the many techniques I learned from him was 4–7–8 breathing. It is also known as the Relaxing Breath Exercise because of its ability to invoke the relaxation response. It is one of the most powerful relaxing breath exercises I have learned. For this reason, I have used it daily and have taught it ever since. In 4-7-8 breathing, students are invited to gently shift their breathing pattern or rhythm for four cycles in order to invoke the relaxation response. The numbers in the name refer to the count when they are breathing in (4), holding their breath (7), and breathing out (8). The speed with which these numbers are counted is not important as it may be different for everyone. It is the ratio that counts. Used over time, it can help students transition from a labored and stressful type of breathing to a more relaxed breathing rhythm. After a few guided practice rounds, students can learn to do this technique on their own when needed.

1. Write *4–7–8* on chart paper or on the board for students to see as they count through.

2. Write the words *Breathe In* above the number 4, the word *Hold* above the number 7 and the words *Breathe Out* above the number 8.

3. Remind students they will breathe in through their nose and breathe out through their mouth.

4. Invite students into the practice:

> *Begin by exhaling all of your breath out through your mouth.*
> *With your mouth closed, inhale through your nose for a count of four.*
> *Hold your breath for a count of seven.*
> *Exhale through your mouth for a count of eight. As you exhale you should make a whooshing sound.*
> *Again, breathe in through your nose for a count of four.*
> *Hold for seven.*
> *Breathe out for eight.*
> *Repeat this two more times for a total of four cycles.*

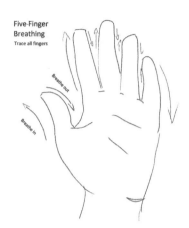

Five-Finger Breathing
Trace all fingers

Breathe out

Breathe in

5. Invite students to Think–Pair–Share about how they felt before 4–7–8 Breathing and how they feel afterward.

Five-Finger Breathing

Five-finger breathing is a mindfulness technique that gives students a visual cue to help them focus their attention on their breathing for five cycles of in-and-out breathing. The use of the hand helps anchor students' attention to focusing on their breath. After a few guided practice rounds, students can learn to do this technique on their own when needed. I have seen students elect to use this technique when they have needed a grounding moment. For younger children, it might help to begin with tracing (see activity sheet on page 54) and then graduate to using their own hand.

1. Let students know they will be using one of their hands and the index finger on their other hand to do something called Five-finger breathing.
2. Ask students to raise their writing hands in the air. Have them fold all of their fingers down except for the pointer finger. This should now look like they are pointing to the ceiling. Model this for your students.
3. Let them know they will be using this finger to trace the fingers of their other hand.
4. Model Five-finger breathing for your students: place your index finger at the bottom of your thumb of your other hand; inhale as you slowly trace your index finger up the outside of your thumb; when you reach the top of your thumb, exhale through your mouth and trace your index finger down the inside of your thumb until you touch the space between your thumb and your index finger; continue to inhale and exhale as you make your way up and down each of the rest of your fingers.
5. Invite students into the practice:

    Start with your non-writing hand in a high-five position. Take the index finger of your writing hand and place it at the bottom of your thumb on your high-five hand. Your index finger should be at the top of your wrist and just below your thumb. Inhale as you slowly trace your index finger up the outside of your thumb.

    When you reach the top of your thumb, exhale through your mouth and trace your index finger down the inside of your thumb until you touch the space between your thumb and your index finger.

    Now continue to inhale and exhale as you make your way across each of the rest of your fingers.

    When you reach the end of your pinky finger, start over at the bottom of your thumb.

    Do this several times until you hear the sound of the bell.

6. You can invite students to complete the Five-Finger Breathing activity sheet on page 54. This activity sheet provides a template with directions and a space for students to record their experiences.

Voice from the Classroom: Mindful Breathing
by Shira Wolch

Every teacher recognizes the moment in the classroom when anxiety fills the room. It's almost physical. The air gets thicker and the noise level rises, as does the temperature. It might occur after a conflict-filled recess, or when a new and challenging task has been assigned (perhaps without enough scaffolding). Often it is related to group-work scenarios. This unease is contagious, hopping from one student to another, their demeanors changing as it does. Three years ago in my classroom, these episodes of heightened anxiety seemed to be happening more and more frequently. I wasn't sure if it was my teaching style, the content of my lessons, or simply "kids these days." What I did know was that I needed to do something about it. That is when I turned to mindfulness.

Although I had learned about mindfulness in teacher's college, it wasn't until my third year of teaching that I turned to it as a practice for myself. I was confronted by a number of obstacles in my own life and I had my most challenging group of students to date. After just a few weeks of regular meditation practice, the stresses of both school and life became more manageable. When I saw the difference mindfulness made in my own life, I hoped it would be helpful for my increasingly agitated students.

In my second-grade classroom we had two dedicated time periods within the school day to practice mindfulness. The first, a shared mindfulness meditation, took place in the morning after students completed their bell work. This lasted 2–5 minutes, no longer. I turned off the lights; the students closed their eyes, backs straight, feet on the floor, hands on their knees. I rang our mindfulness bell and walked the students through a brief guided mediation. For the first few weeks, meditation focused on breathing. We then moved on to visualizations. Through these exercises, students were learning to help themselves self-regulate when their emotions overwhelmed them.

The second mindfulness practice occurred after lunch recess—often a very emotional time of day (depending on who won the soccer game). At this time, I simply rang the bell; we closed our eyes and took 10 deep breaths. This cooled us down, calmed our emotions from recess, and allowed us a fresh start on learning.

I found that the most successful way to teach mindfulness strategies was to be overt with my teaching. I complemented the meditation practices with information about how the brain functions. For example, I had one student who struggled with outbursts of anger, including throwing furniture, hitting his peers, tearing up his work, and more. His triggers were completely unknown to himself and to me. I started teaching him how anger is triggered in the brain, and exploring the idea of neuroplasticity. When he understood that he simply needed to create a new neural pathway for when he was "set off," it became an achievable goal. We set out a plan to create new neural pathways together. Whenever he got angry he would sit in a corner alone and count his breaths. Initially he would count to the 1000s, then the 100s; eventually just walking to the corner for a few seconds was enough to calm him down. He had conditioned himself to not react with violence, but rather with deep breathing. Mindfulness changed his reactions, which eventually affected many other parts of his school life and relationships.

Like any other new skill, repetition was critical. For every new strategy I taught students, we practiced 3–5 times in the first week, then once or twice a month after that. One of the first strategies I taught was circle breathing. Students drew a circle in the air in front of them; the top of the circle represented an inhalation, and the bottom an exhalation. Simple. Concrete. Effective. As the students drew big slow circles, they took big deep breaths. After learning this skill, we discussed when this strategy might come in handy. I noted their ideas on chart paper. Later in the week I practiced circle breathing with students three more times. Following each meditation, I ran through a quick recap of when we could use our circle breaths. Later on, if a situation occurred in class in which this practice would be helpful, I could remind students to take a few circle breaths or practice their circle breathing until they were feeling calm. The common language and familiarity of the strategy made it easy for them to do independently. Once I saw a child drawing circles in the air during a standardized test. My heart soared—another mindfulness success.

Small yet significant changes began to occur for my students. Parents started to let me know that their children were beginning to use the strategies at home. One student asked for a mindful moment before going into the dentist's office. Another student had a mindful moment before completing their homework. Another used mindfulness to help her fall asleep at night. By mid-February, I had a parent tell me about her child who was in the middle of an argument with her sibling when she abruptly left and walked into her room. She spent ten minutes with her "mindfulness jar," calmed herself, and returned to talk things through with her sibling. This parent said to me, "How is my seven-year-old more rational than I am?" This is exactly why we practice! I want my students to learn how to stop, breathe, reevaluate, then respond.

As I move on to a new group of students each year, I realize a few of my students may opt out of our daily practice at first. More of these students end up joining than not. What I am confident about is that, if I am consistent about including mindfulness in the classroom, I will be giving my students the strategies to help themselves. As a result, they will be better able to self-regulate, enjoy school, develop deep relationships, and gain increased self-awareness. I've seen what's possible.

Thoughts as Clouds

Name: _____   Date: _____

Imagine thoughts are like passing clouds and you are watching them go by. What thoughts came and went when you tried mindfulness? Draw or use words.

Writing Prompt after Mindful Breathing: K–Grade 2

Name: _____   Date: _____

How did you feel BEFORE mindfulness? Color or circle.

How do you feel AFTER mindfulness? Color or circle.

Use pictures or words to describe what it was like to try Mindful Breathing.

Pembroke Publishers ©2019 *Fostering Mindfulness* by Shelley Murphy ISBN 978-1-55138-340-8

Writing Prompt after Mindful Breathing: Grades 3–6

Name: _____   Date: _____

You have just tried a mindful breathing practice. Think about and respond to the questions below. You may respond by writing and/or drawing.

Which mindful breathing practice did you try?

How did you feel before mindfulness?

How do you feel after mindfulness?

In what ways might this help you throughout the rest of the day?

Pembroke Publishers ©2019 *Fostering Mindfulness* by Shelley Murphy ISBN 978-1-55138-340-8

Back-to-Back Mindful Breathing: K–Grade 2

Name: _____   Date: _____

You just practiced Back-to-Back Mindful Breathing with a partner. Use words or images to describe what you noticed and how you felt during Back-to-Back Mindful Breathing.

Pembroke Publishers ©2019 *Fostering Mindfulness* by Shelley Murphy ISBN 978-1-55138-340-8

Back-to-Back Mindful Breathing: Grades 3–6

Name: _____   Date: _____

You just practiced Back-to-Back Mindful Breathing with a partner. Take a few moments to think about and answer the following questions:

How did it feel to practice Back-to-Back Mindful Breathing with a partner?

What did you notice about the rhythm or pattern of your breathing compared to your partner's breathing? Was it faster? Slower? Were you able to match your partner's breathing pattern?

What did you learn about your own breathing?

Use words or images to describe how you felt during this mindfulness practice.

Square Breathing

Name: _____   Date: _____

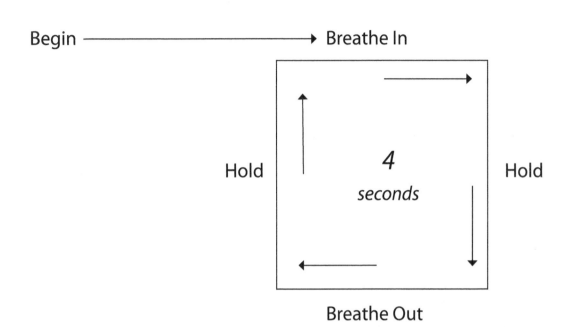

For Square Breathing you can use this box to trace your finger along the lines as you breathe in, hold, breathe out, and hold again. Be sure to start where it says "Begin". What did you notice about your breathing as you tried this exercise? How did it make your mind and your body feel? Use the space below.

Five-Finger Breathing

Name: _____   Date: _____

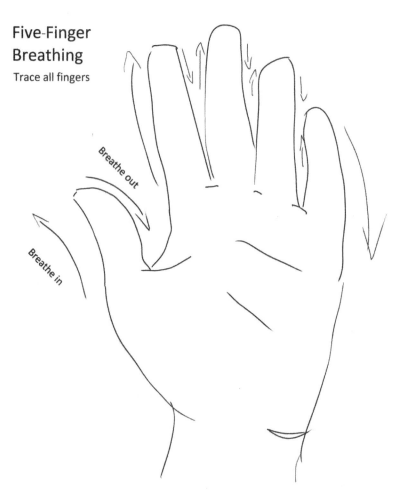

Five-Finger
Breathing
Trace all fingers

Breathe out

Breathe in

What did you notice about your breathing as you tried this exercise? How did it make your mind and your body feel? Use the space below.

Pembroke Publishers ©2019 *Fostering Mindfulness* by Shelley Murphy ISBN 978-1-55138-340-8

4

Mindfulness and the Five Senses

What Is Mindful Sensing?

"In truth we are always present; we only imagine ourselves to be in one place or another."
— Howard Cohn

Our senses are the main tools we use to perceive the world. As we go about our busy lives, most of us use each of our five senses—sight, hearing, smell, taste, and touch—almost unconsciously. In general, we do not pay close and mindful attention to each of our senses as we go about our daily lives. We can invite our students, however, to use their senses to help develop their mindful attention. Mindful sensing involves paying purposeful attention to one sense at a time. You can take students through a mindfulness exercise that isolates one sense or you can take a tour of some or all five of the senses. Either way, you are inviting students to use their senses as an anchor (just as they did with their breath) to connect and reconnect with the present moment.

Mindful sensing gives students an opportunity to strengthen their ability to direct their attention to a task at hand and to redirect their attention when something distracts it away. Actually, our minds have a mechanism that helps us to navigate our senses while keeping our attention where we want and need it to be. Our brains have something called the RAS, or reticular activation system. It acts like a filter for most of the sensory input coming at it from our environment. This part of the brain is often compared to a gatekeeper or executive assistant. Just as an executive assistant decides which phone calls get screened out and which ones get through, the role of the RAS is to make sure we do not take in more sensory information than we can handle. Research in neuroscience shows that our senses take in millions of bits of data per second, but our brains can process only around 40 pieces of data per second. This is an incredibly small percentage. So the role of the RAS is to decide which data/information should be brought into the conscious mind and what information can be safely ignored.

Think of your own experience as you read this. It is likely there is a lot of competing sensory information in your current environment—the hum of the lights or sounds of traffic, the smell of lunch, the feel of your clothes against your skin, the sight of people or objects around you, the distant taste of coffee or a recent snack. All these sensory experiences are wired directly to and through the RAS. Your RAS is helping you to safely ignore some of the sensory information coming at you as you read this, helping keep your mind focused and alert. Right now, your RAS is alerting your brain that messages are on the way through your sense of sight and it's alerting the rest of your senses not to send any conflicting messages until your brain is free to get back to them. At times your brain may be temporarily diverted from the visual sensation involved in reading (by the sound of a loud bang or baby crying) but, for the most part, your RAS is helping to make sure you can direct and redirect your attention back to the page.

We can help to strengthen our students' RAS by giving them opportunities to practice being intentional about directing their attention to one or all of their senses. This also strengthens their ability to regulate their attention towards the present moment and on the task at hand. As students strengthen their RAS, they strengthen their capacity to direct their attention where they want it to be and to keep it there.

Tips for Teaching Mindful Sensing

- Mindful sensing activities can be integrated into the classroom schedule in just a few moments a day.
- Activities can be modified, shortened, or lengthened as appropriate for grade level.
- As with many mindfulness activities, mindful sensing activities begin and end with students noticing their bodies and turning their awareness to their breath.
- Apart from for mindful seeing, it's often easier for students to pay careful attention to their experiences when their eyes are closed.
- As students become familiar and comfortable with mindful sensing, they can be invited to focus on one or all of their senses for just one minute during the day when a moment of calm is needed.
- Children with ASD often have either a heightened or reduced sensory response through one or more of their five senses.

Introducing Sensory Awareness

Tapping into the Senses

This lesson introduces students to the five senses in preparation for mindful sensing activities. It provides a grade-appropriate overview of the function and purpose of each sense.

1. Copy and display individual Sense Cards found on pages 70–72.
2. Use the Tapping Into Our Senses activity sheet on pages 73–75. The first page of the activity sheet for K–Grade 2 is different from the first page for Grades 3–6; the second page is the same for both grade ranges. The first page of the activity sheet provides a grade-appropriate explanation of each of the senses; the second page provides a space for students to consider and write about how they have used each of their senses in a given day.

In addition to providing mindfulness practices for the five senses, this chapter includes mindful eating, which is often considered a core mindfulness practice.

Sense Cards can be used in a pocket chart when leading small groups or the whole class through mindful-sensing activities. They can also be placed at stations, in the Peace Corner, or at individual or clustered desks.

This introductory lesson is optional.

Senses cards from pages 70–72 can be printed on heavy paper, such as cardstock, and can be laminated. Of course, they work just as well on simple copy paper.

3. To draw on background knowledge, point to each of the Sense Cards and have students Think–Pair–Share how they are using their senses right now. Invite one or two students to share for the whole class.
4. Distribute the first page of Tapping into Our Senses activity sheet and use it to review the role and purpose of each of the senses.
5. Invite students to complete the second page of the activity sheet, which asks them to think more deeply about their experience of using each of their senses.
6. Invite a few students to share responses with whole group.

Individual Senses

Sense of Smell

Our most powerful sense is our sense of smell, yet we often don't notice the smells around us until they become extreme. Mindful smelling invites students to intentionally activate and focus on their sense of smell. Students are guided through focusing their awareness on their sense of smell. This can be done by simply using the natural smell in the air (even if it's neutral). You can also tap into students' sense of smell by bringing some familiar scents into the classroom to play a guess-that-smell game (small jars or paper cups filled with scented items, such as cinnamon, lavender, vinegar, coffee, banana, orange peel, scented soap, essential oils, peppermint, etc.). It is important to be aware that some students might be sensitive to certain scents.

smell

Use scripts as a guide. You may read as-is or modify to fit your needs.

1. Invite students into the practice:

   Let your body get comfortable in your chair or on the floor. Sit with your back straight and let your shoulders drop. Imagine there is a string at the top of your head and it's pulling your back up a little straighter. Both feet are touching the ground and your hands are on your lap. Gently close your eyes and turn your attention to your sense of smell. Really focus on what you can smell. If you don't smell anything, that's okay. Just be aware of this. When you notice that you are no longer focusing on your sense of smell, this means your mind has wandered. Bring your awareness back to your sense of smell. Continue to rest your awareness on your experience of smell until you hear the sound of the bell and it recedes.

2. You can invite students students to write or draw what they noticed during mindful smelling and to record what it was like for them to use their sense mindfully.

Sense of Hearing

hearing

In mindful hearing (listening), students are guided through focusing their awareness on their sense of hearing. They may be asked to be still and quiet, and to listen to the sounds around them. Students often note the hum of the lights, the sound of their classmates breathing, children on the playground or in the hallways, the sound of cars driving by outside their school window, the school announcement over the PA system, etc. Students may also be asked to listen to deliberately created sounds, to play listening games, or to listen mindfully to a partner.

The Environment

1. Invite students into the practice:

   Let your body get comfortable in your chair or on the floor. Sit with your back straight and let your shoulders drop. Imagine there is a string at the top of your head and it's pulling your back up a little straighter. Both feet are touching the ground and your hands are on your lap. Gently close your eyes and turn your attention to the sounds around you. Really focus on what you can hear from outside of the room and from inside of the room. When you notice that you are no longer focusing on your sense of hearing, this means your mind has wandered. Bring your awareness back to your sense of hearing. Continue to rest your awareness on your experience of hearing until you hear the sound of the bell and it recedes.

2. You can invite students to write or draw what they noticed during mindful hearing and to record what it was like for them to use their sense mindfully.

Mystery Sound

For more on the RAS, see page 55.

In this activity, students are asked to listen to deliberately created sounds and to guess what the source is. Share with students that, in addition to being fun, this activity helps to strengthen the part of their brain that will help them to be better listeners. For older students, explain that it helps to strengthen the RAS.

1. Gather objects that make distinct sounds; e.g., click of a ballpoint pen, bells, drums, shakers, crinkling of paper, coins, bouncing ball, keys, etc.
2. Place objects in a cardboard box or thick bag so students are unable to see them. Invite students to close their eyes or face away from you on their chairs.
3. You can use the Mystery Sound activity sheet on page 76 or 77 for students to record their guesses.
4. Invite students to focus on their breathing for a few in and out cycles (30 seconds).
5. Ask students to listen very carefully to each of the sounds so they can to try to identify what it is. Students should be instructed not to call out.
6. Begin making a sound with one of your mystery objects; continue for 5–10 seconds.
7. Put the object out of sight and ask students to open their eyes and record what they believe the mystery object is.
8. Continue steps 6 and 7 with the remaining objects.
9. Have students Think–Pair–Share their Mystery Sound guesses.
10. To conclude, show each of the objects in the order they were presented.

ABC Game

This is a fun and engaging way to invite students into mindfulness practice using the alphabet. You or one of the students can begin saying "A" out loud. Any of the other students can elect to say the letter "B" out loud, and so on. If two students say their letters at the same time, the group must start over at "A." Any student can elect to begin again. The object of the game is to get as far into the alphabet as possible without having to start over. This game can go on for as short or as long a time as you would like. In this activity, students are listening mindfully for someone else to say a letter; they are practicing how to notice their responses (e.g., frustration, anger, happiness) without being drawn into them. You may also do this activity with numbers instead of letters.

1. Students can be seated at their desks, standing, or sitting on the carpet. Invite students to close their eyes or lower their chins, and look down.
2. Let students know they may get frustrated with having to start the alphabet over a number of times. Invite them to notice what they are feeling. This is part of the mindfulness practice.
3. Invite students into the practice:

    Let your body get comfortable in your chair or on the floor. Sit with your back straight and let your shoulders drop. Imagine there is a string at the top of your head and it's pulling your back up a little straighter. Both feet are touching the ground and your hands are on your lap.

    Now turn your attention to your sense of hearing. In a moment, we're going to begin the ABC Game. In this game, I'll begin by saying the letter "A." Then someone else will say the letter "B." You do not have to be invited or raise your hand. Just call out the letter out. No one knows who will say the next letter and that's how it should be.

    Continue moving along the alphabet until two people say one letter at the same time. This will probably happen. When this happens, we start back at the letter "A." You might have to start over and over again, and that's expected. Your job is to listen mindfully to whoever is saying a letter (that could also be you) and notice your thoughts when two people say the letter at the same time and we have to start over. Notice what's on your mind. You might feel frustration or anger, and that's okay. Just notice these feelings and then bring your attention back to listening to your classmates saying the letters. Let's begin.

4. Continue the ABC Game for 1 minute.
5. Ask students to Think–Pair–Share their experience of playing the ABC Game and to name challenging feelings, such as frustration, anger, etc., that might have arisen during the game.
6. Let students know they will be playing the ABC Game a second time. This time, if feelings of frustration or anger or sadness arise, ask them to simply notice those feelings and bring their attention back to listening to the sounds of people calling out the alphabet.
7. Play the ABC Game for 1–3 minutes.
8. Have students Think–Pair–Share their experience of the second round of the ABC Game; ask them to share if they were able to notice their feelings rather than be drawn into them.

Mindful Listening with a Partner

Listening is a fundamental goal in many language arts programs, yet it is often the least understood, taught, and practiced language skill in school. While students spend years learning how to read and write, very little focus is given to teaching the important skill of listening. We imagine listening to be a natural skill. Actually, it requires intention, attention, and practice. This is becoming increasingly more challenging for our students as they are immersed in a culture of distraction. As Stephen Covey has written: "Most people do not listen with the intent to understand; they listen with the intent to reply" (Covey 1989). This is because, regardless of our intent, our minds tend to wander and our inner dialogue often hijacks our attention away from truly listening. Our own narratives, biases, thoughts, and perspectives related to what the person is saying start to take over. To listen mindfully takes practice; over time, it is a skill that can be strengthened.

Students generally love this activity. They come to understand how to be a more thoughtful, present, and empathetic listener. They also experience what it feels like to be truly listened to, which helps improve mutual understanding and trust. As one student said, "It feels like an act of care and love. When someone truly listens to us we feel it and know it."

1. Get students into partners and have them face each other. Use the entire space of your classroom so partners are as far apart from other students as possible.
2. Let students know they will each be taking a turn speaking while their partner listens to them for a length of time between 2–5 minutes; this will vary by grade level (e.g., 5 minutes for Grades 4–6).
3. Remind students that this is a mindfulness practice. That means they are using what their partner is saying as an object of focus. When their minds inevitably wander, it means they are no longer connected to the present. They should be instructed simply to bring their attention back to the present by listening once again to the words of the person speaking.
4. Ask partners to decide who will be the first listener and who will be the first speaker. Ask listeners to raise their hands. Prompt students in the listening role to listen only. This means they must be silent but attentive. There should be no talking and no audible sounds. This can often be quite challenging for students who are used to the ebb and flow of a natural conversation. The inherent challenge in this exercise is what makes it a valuable mindfulness practice.
5. Ask speakers to raise their hands. Prompt students in the speaking role to speak for as much of the allotted time as possible. Many students share experiences or concerns with their partners. If speaking students run out of things to share, prompt partners to hold the space with silence. This often means neither of the partners is speaking; tell them that's okay.
6. Once students understand the instructions, start the timer for 2–5 minutes.
7. Once the timer has gone off to signal the end of the first partner's opportunity to practice mindful listening, have students switch roles.
8. Start the timer for 2–5 minutes once more.
9. Once the timer has gone off, and before allowing students to debrief about their conversation, invite students to share their thoughts about what it was like to be in the mindful listener role or the speaker role.
10. You can invite students to complete the Be a Mindful Listener activity sheet on page 78, to share what it was like for them to speak and be listened to mindfully.
11. You can give students a few minutes to debrief about what was shared during their Mindful Listening activity with their partners. Students often need a moment or two to comment on or ask questions about what was shared.

I do not give students an opportunity to debrief between listening sessions, as I want them to uphold the mindful environment. I often invite students to debrief at the end.

Voice from the Classroom: Mindful Listening
by Dakota Panacci

Each day my students would enter the classroom buzzing with energy from recess. Every conversation, game, fight, or thought experienced out at recess came back into the classroom with them. The playground seemed to bring out stress and anxiety in many of my students. This was especially difficult for my students with special education needs and behavior challenges; it made learning quite difficult. In truth, many of my students had aggressive behaviors, both verbal and physical, with few coping strategies to help them self-regulate. Our goal with mindfulness practice was to provide a tool to help them calm down and refocus before behaviors escalated in a way that would be harmful to themselves or others. We wanted students to focus on listening or breathing patterns and use them to de-escalate.

Over time we established a routine of mindfulness practice to follow a major transition into the classroom. For 10–15 minutes, we use mindful listening and breathing to teach de-escalation strategies. Students typically participate in two listening activities.

In the first activity, students choose a sound they want to focus on for their mindful listening and breathing exercise for the day. They choose from birds chirping, waterfalls, rain falling, or leaves rustling. As students walk into the classroom, they are invited to find a quiet space. Some sit on a chair with their feet flat on the ground and their hands in their laps, while others lie on the floor with their feet out straight and their toes toward the ceiling. Once the room falls silent, students begin by focusing on the different sounds in the room. Eventually, we play their chosen sound and they direct their focus there. The bell rings and students are asked to focus on each inhalation and each exhalation of their breath. Over time, the length of the listening and breathing activity gets longer, moving from three to ten minutes. At the sound of the second bell, students are asked to open their eyes, wiggle their fingers and toes, and quietly sit up. As students sit up and show their readiness to begin their learning, we begin to move to our academic tasks.

In the second activity, students sit with their eyes closed at their desk or on the carpet. One student comes to the front of the room and quietly makes a noise using classroom objects or clothing. They may run their zipper up their sweater, tap a marker on the whiteboard, or scratch their nail on the carpet. Students who are seated are asked to guess the noise that was made. When a student guesses correctly they come to the front of the room and complete the activity once again. This particular practice happens right after recess during mindfulness practice and throughout the day when students need a break to refocus.

This has supported my students in many ways. David is a student who often exhibited verbal and physical aggression toward staff and students. At the beginning of the year he would yell, throw objects, and get physical with those around him. One day, David became extremely frustrated after losing a board game. As a class team we could sense the potential for aggressive behavior and gave David some space. By this time, David had been practicing mindfulness for most of the year. David sat quietly at a table and, after a few minutes, I approached him to ask if he wanted to continue to play. As he sat with his fists clenched tightly he said, "I'm not ready... I want to sit here and listen to Caleb play his game." I left David at the table and, over the course of a few minutes, he unclenched his fists, calmed himself, stood up, and went back to join his classmates.

Mindfulness practice has become an integral part of my teaching day. Like David, many students have found and commented that these activities help them control their emotions and behaviors because they give them tools to refocus their energy. It helps to support their ability to self-regulate both in and out of the classroom.

touch

Sense of Touch

Our students' bodies are often touching something, but most of the time they are unaware of it. Using their sense of touch as a form of mindfulness, students can direct their attention and awareness toward whatever comes into contact with their body. It could be their body in contact with the floor, their chair, or their desk; their clothes against their skin; the temperature around them; etc. They may be asked to choose a particular object to focus their sense of touch on.

Sense of Body

1. Invite students into the practice:

    Let your body get comfortable in your chair or on the floor. Sit with your back straight and let your shoulders drop. Imagine there is a string at the top of your head and it's pulling your back up a little straighter. Both feet are touching the ground and your hands are on your lap.

    Turn your attention to whatever sense of touch comes into your awareness. You may notice your feet coming in contact with the floor or the feel of the chair against your back. You might notice your hands resting on your lap, your arms against the sides of your body, or your lips resting against each other. You may notice the feel of your clothes against your skin or the temperature in the room. Just stay with any sensations of touch. When you notice you are no longer focusing on your sense of touch, this means your mind has wandered. Bring your attention back to your awareness of touch and continue to rest your awareness there until you hear the sound of the bell and it recedes.

2. You can invite students to write or draw what they noticed during the mindful touch practice and to record what it was like for them to use their sense mindfully.

Sense of an Object

1. Be sure to have students choose an object to focus their sense of touch on: e.g., eraser, book, pencil, fidget tool, etc.
2. Invite students into the practice:

    Let your body get comfortable in your chair or on the floor. Sit with your back straight and let your shoulders drop. Imagine there is a string at the top of your head and it's pulling your back up a little straighter. Both feet are touching the ground and your hands are on your lap.

    Turn your awareness/attention to the object in your hands. Notice how the object feels within your hand. What textures do you notice? Does your object feel warm? Cold? Just stay with the sensations of touch. When you notice that you are no longer focusing on your sense of touch, this means your mind has wandered. Bring your awareness back to your experience of touch and continue to rest it there until you hear the sound of the bell and it recedes.

3. You can invite students to write or draw what they noticed during the mindful touch practice and to record what it was like for them to use their sense mindfully.

Sense of Taste

taste

Using the sense of taste as a form of mindfulness can be done in two ways. Students can be asked to focus their sense of taste within their mouth as it is, or they can be invited to engage in a mindful eating exercise with a raisin or other food (see Mindful Eating on page 66). Either way, they are asked to purposefully focus their attention on their sense of taste.

1. Invite students into the practice:

   Let your body get comfortable in your chair or on the floor. Sit with your back straight and let your shoulders drop. Imagine there is a string at the top of your head and it's pulling your back up a little straighter. Both feet are touching the ground and your hands are on your lap.

   Now turn your attention to your sense of taste. Notice the taste within your mouth, just as it is here and now. You might sense a bit of sweetness or bitterness, or it could be a neutral taste. It doesn't really matter what you are sensing. What's important is that you are simply focusing your awareness on the taste in your mouth, even if it's neutral or there is no taste. When you notice that you are no longer focusing on what you taste, that means your mind has wandered. Bring your awareness back to any sensations of taste. Continue to rest your awareness on your experience of taste until you hear the sound of the bell and it recedes.

2. You can invite students to write or draw what they noticed during the mindful taste practice and to record what it was like for them to use their sense mindfully.

Sense of Sight

sight

Using the sense of sight as a mindfulness practice can be done in a number of different ways. Students can be invited to observe their surroundings and notice what captures their visual attention. They can be invited to observe the general surrounding of the room or area, or to focus their awareness on one specific object.

The Environment

1. Invite students into the practice:

   Let your body get comfortable in your chair or on the floor. Sit with your back straight and let your shoulders drop. Imagine there is a string at the top of your head and it's pulling your back up a little straighter. Both feet are touching the ground and your hands are on your lap.

   Now shift your awareness to your sense of sight. Take notice of any colors, shapes, and textures throughout the room. Remember not to get caught up in analyzing what you see. Just rest your awareness on what your eyes see for the next few moments. Because you are looking so mindfully, you may notice something that you've never noticed before.

   When you notice that you are no longer focusing on what you see, that means your mind has wandered. Bring your awareness back to what you see in the room. Continue to rest your awareness on your experience of vision until you hear the sound of the bell and it recedes.

2. You can invite students to write or draw what they noticed during the mindful seeing practice and to record what it was like for them to use their sense mindfully.

Sense of an Object

1. Invite students to choose a small object from the classroom to focus on for this sense of sight practice.
2. Invite students into the practice:

    Let your body get comfortable in your chair or on the floor. Sit with your back straight and let your shoulders drop. Imagine there is a string at the top of your head and it's pulling your back up a little straighter. Both feet are touching the ground and your hands are on your lap.

    Now shift your awareness to your sense of sight. Take notice of the details of your object. Notice what catches your eye. It could be its color or colors, its brightness, the shape of it, etc. Remember not to get caught up in analyzing what you see. Just rest your awareness on what your eyes see for the next few moments. Because you are looking so mindfully, you may notice something that you've never noticed before.

    When you notice that you are no longer focusing on what you see, that means your mind has wandered. Bring your awareness back to what you see in the room. Continue to rest your awareness on your experience of vision until you hear the sound of the bell and it recedes.

3. You can invite students to write or draw what they noticed during the mindful seeing practice and to record what it was like for them to use their sense mindfully.

All Five Senses

Five-Senses Tour

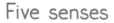

Five senses

touch   smell   taste

hearing

sight

In this five-senses mindfulness exercise, students are guided through a tour of their senses and invited to pay attention to whatever comes into their awareness through each sense. You might want to let students know they are not doing it wrong if they are not able to detect through all of their senses. For example, they may not sense a smell or a taste as they take their tour. The goal is to simply be aware of whatever sensations they notice in the moment without labelling or judging those sensations good or bad. You can spend anywhere from 30 seconds to two minutes on each sense, depending on the age, grade, and attention span of your students.

The goal is for students to describe their experience rather than to label or judge it:

Description: *I hear the sound of a clock ticking; I feel the chair against my back; I see a bird flying outside the window; I smell nothing.*
Judgment or label: *this tastes good; this feels bad; I don't like that smell; I like seeing and birds in trees.*

1. Invite students into the practice:

    Let your body get comfortable in your chair or on the floor. Sit with your back straight and let your shoulders drop. Imagine there is a string at the top of your head and it's pulling your back up a little straighter. Both feet are touching the ground and your hands are on your lap.

You are going to start by taking a nice deep breath in through your nose and out through your mouth. Let's do this two more times. Breathe in through your nose and breathe out through your mouth. One more time: breathe in through your nose and breathe out through your mouth. Now keep your attention on your breathing and let your breath find its own rhythm.

Let's begin by turning your attention to five things you can see. Is there anything in the room you haven't noticed before? You might become aware of the colors and shapes of objects, or even lights or marks on the wall that you didn't notice before. Choose five things to really see.
(Pause for 30 seconds to one minute)

2. Continue the lesson:

   Once you've done that, shift your attention to noticing five things you can hear. It might be helpful to close your eyes for the rest of this exercise. What do you hear from outside of the room? What you hear from inside of the room?
   (Pause for 30 seconds to one minute)

3. Continue the lesson:

   Now shift your awareness to five things you currently feel with your sense of touch. You might feel the floor as your feet or body rests on it. You might feel the clothes against your skin, your hands resting on your lap, or the feel of your back against the chair. Just notice what you are feeling with your sense of touch.
   (Pause for 30 seconds to one minute)

4. Continue the lesson:

   Now shift your awareness again and notice what you can taste. You might still taste something you had for breakfast or lunch or at recess, or you may not taste anything at all. That's okay. What's important is that you are focusing your attention on your sense of taste—even if there is no taste.
   (Pause for 30 seconds to one minute)

5. Continue the lesson:

   Now shift your awareness one last time to notice what you can smell. Bring your awareness to anything you notice. If you don't smell anything, that's okay too. Just notice that.
   (Pause for 30 seconds to one minute)

6. Conclude the lesson:

   So now, turn your attention back to your breathing. Notice the rise and fall of your belly as you breathe in and as you breathe out. Let's do that for a few more breaths.
   (Pause)
   I'll ring the bell, and when you can no longer hear the sound of it, open your eyes.

7. You can invite students to complete the Five Senses Tour activity sheet on page 79, to write or draw what they noticed during the Five Senses Tour and to record what it was like for them to use their five senses mindfully.

Mindful Eating

Mindful eating invites students to eat with mindful attention by engaging all of their senses. Like a scientist, they will use their senses to see, listen to, smell, touch, and taste their food. Mindfulness learned in relation to eating can influence how consciously children eat in their daily lives. Many students (and adults) eat food quickly and on autopilot. Before we have finished chewing and swallowing one spoonful or forkful of food, we are bringing another and then another to our mouths without even thinking about it. By bringing complete awareness to the food through their senses, students are learning to direct their attention where they want it to be and to be more mindful and appreciative of food's various characteristics. Mindful eating can also help students develop a healthier relationship with food and can be particularly helpful for students dealing with anxiety related to food, eating, or body image.

For this exercise, students are invited to eat one piece of food as they normally would and another piece of food very, very slowly. Any food will do, as long as it is portioned into a small size. While small pieces of chocolate or orange pieces are popular with my students, raisins are most often used. I have done this exercise with hundreds of students using just two tiny raisins each. This is often a very powerful experience for students. Almost invariably, after a mindful-eating exercise a student will proclaim something like, "I eat raisins all of the time but it never felt like this!"

1. If possible, begin by asking students to wash or sanitize their hands.
2. Place two raisins on a piece of tissue or paper towel on each student's desk. Be sure to instruct them not to touch their raisins until they are invited to do so. (Be prepared to replace a few, as they will often disappear anyway!)
3. Invite students to eat one raisin as they typically would. As they do this, model eating the raisin yourself.
4. Once the first raisin has been eaten (and this usually happens quite quickly), invite students into the practice:

    We are now going to try something called mindful eating with your second raisin. Be sure to leave your raisin on your desk for now. This will be very different from how you usually eat. Mindful eating gives you a chance to act like a scientist. You will use your senses to see, listen to, smell, touch, and taste your food.

    Let your body get comfortable in your chair and let your shoulders drop. Relax your jaw and let your mouth open just slightly. Imagine there is a string at the top of your head and it's pulling your back up just a little straighter. Both feet are touching the ground and your hands are on your belly or your lap. Let's start with three nice deep breaths. Breathe in through your nose and breathe out through your mouth.
    (Pause)
    Now breathe naturally and notice your belly rising and falling.
    (Pause)
    We are now going to begin mindful eating.

    Look at the raisin on your desk. Imagine you are a scientist and you are seeing a raisin for the very first time. Lift it up and take a very careful look at it. What do you see? What do you notice about its color? It's size? Its shape? Do you see any bumps or ridges? Hold it up to the light to see if you notice anything different about its color or shape. Do you notice any sensations in your mouth as you look at it?
    (Pause for a few seconds)

Now close your eyes and turn your attention to your sense of touch. How does the raisin feel in your hand? Feel the weight of it. Now begin to gently roll it around with your fingers. How does it feel? Do you feel any bumps or ridges? Is it warm or cool? Does the texture or temperature change as you roll it around?

Now bring your raisin up to your nose to use your sense of smell. Keep your eyes closed. Have you ever smelled a raisin before? What do you notice? What do you smell? You may start to think this is a funny thing to do. That's okay. Just notice these thoughts and then bring your attention back to your raisin.

Now bring your raisin up to one of your ears to use your sense of hearing. Keep your eyes closed and be as still and quiet as you can. Again, this might feel like a funny thing to do, and that's okay. Just notice these thoughts and then bring your attention back to the raisin beside your ear. Use your fingers to roll it around beside your ear. Does your raisin make a sound? What do you hear?

Now you're going to use your sense of taste. Without biting into your raisin, place it on your tongue. Don't start to chew your raisin yet. Do you notice anything happening in your mouth or in your stomach as the raisin sits on your tongue? Do you taste anything yet? Can you feel bumps or ridges? Does it feel warm? Notice if you have any urges to start chewing.

Now slowly bite into your raisin and become aware of what you taste and hear and how it feels. Is this different from when it was just sitting on your tongue? Notice what is happening in your mouth. What flavor do you taste? Notice how the raisin feels as you chew it. Notice when your brain sends a message that it's time to finish chewing and to begin swallowing your raisin. Notice how it feels as you chew and then swallow. Imagine your raisin is travelling down your throat and into your stomach. Notice any taste that is left in your mouth.

Take a moment now to think about the long journey of your raisins before they before they got to you today. Think of how your raisins started out as grape seeds that grew into a plant that was taken care of by farmworkers who dried the grapes in the sun so they could become your raisins. Think about the workers who designed and made the box or bag to put your raisins in. Think about the truck driver who drove your raisins to the grocery store. Think about the workers at the grocery store unpacking your raisins and putting them on the shelf. Think about your teacher going to the grocery store to buy your raisins. Think about your raisins travelling with your teacher to school. Now think about the journey of your raisin from your desk, to your hand, to your mouth, and into your stomach where it's nourishing you and giving you energy.

Let's finish up by closing our eyes, if they aren't already, and take three nice deep breaths. Breathe in through your nose and out through your mouth. Continue to notice your breath until you hear the sound of the bell and you are ready to open your eyes.

Take a moment to think about what it was like to eat mindfully. Think about how eating your second raisin was different from eating your first.

5. Ask students to Think–Pair–Share how eating their second raisin was different from eating their first.
6. You can invite students to complete the Mindful Eating: Be a Scientist activity sheet on page 80, to write or draw what they noticed during mindful eating and to record what it was like for them to eat mindfully.

Voice from the Classroom: Mindful Sensing
by Sara Aakbari

We often don't appreciate it enough when we are able to hear, smell, see, feel, and taste. This is one reason why I bring mindful sensing into my classroom. I have worked in a number of schools and in various capacities and have seen, at times, what little attention is given to helping students find a sense of calm. Mindful sensing is one way to help them find this.

There are two mindful sensing activities I most often bring to my students. The first is an exploration of the senses through various foods. When exploring mindful sensing using food, I will often choose a different or new food for the children to explore. For example, I once used marshmallows—a favorite with students. The second way I bring students through an exploration of the senses is while in nature. Taking children outdoors to tap into their senses is always a much different experience from practicing within the confines of the classroom walls. When given a choice of mindfulness practice in nature, students will often gravitate towards mindful sensing. I guide them to use each of their senses for a minute or two to take in all that surrounds them.

During this practice, I often will see children with their hands on their chests or bellies to help them keep track of their breathing. I recall one of my students named Jaelyn. He had a very tough time remaining still for longer than a minute or two. But for these moments of mindfulness and mindful sensing, I would see his body relax, his restless arms and legs would become calm, and he would become more present. After one of our mindfulness activities, Jaelyn asked to speak with me afterwards. "Ms. Aakbari", he said, "I heard and felt my heart beating like a drum. First it was really, really fast like *BOOM BOOM BOOM*, then it got slow like *boooom*."

I find that children who have trouble with self-regulation or who have impulse-control challenges are able to regain their sense of calm and assume more responsibility for their actions. I have even had parents speak with me to share how their children will take time to relax and practice mindfulness at home when they begin to feel overwhelmed or overstimulated. I'm happy in provide my students with opportunities to learn how to take ownership of their behavior and their learning. Mindful sensing is one of the ways I do this.

Voice from the Classroom: Mindful Sensing and the Outdoors
by Michael-James Palazzo

As an International Baccalaureate elementary educator, I view each of my students holistically and believe academic content and exploration of the self to be of equal importance. I also believe that the two should not be regarded as separate and distinct from one another. I incorporate mindfulness practices and activities in my classroom schedule. I currently teach 20 Grades 3/4 students at a private Italian immersion IB/Reggio-inspired school in San Francisco. My students love the outdoors and being with nature. Once a week they are fortunate to attend environmental studies class in our outdoor garden, where they often engage in mindfulness activities.

During our unit on ecosystems, we embarked on a field trip to the Olema Valley north of San Francisco. Prior to attending the field trip, students learned about the

important relationship between salmon and redwood trees. They learned about keystone species and food chains found in various ecosystems. During one mindfulness practice, I introduce my students to the chance to become more present with nature and to "sink in" to the ecosystem while sitting alongside Redwood Creek. The activity, which I call A Moment of Silence in Nature, asks them to take a moment to simply listen to any sounds they may hear. After a minute has passed, we reflect as a class on what we hear and how it feels to be silent in the midst of the sounds of nature. Many students comment about feeling at peace. I've also engaged my students in this type of activity in our school garden or at the nearby park after lunch. I find outdoor mindfulness activities as simple as this one to be effective because they ask students to use their senses in a way that helps them arrive at a more meaningful state of wonder and peace.

Another outdoor mindfulness practice I find especially effective for my hands-on learners and fidgeters is the creation of nature mandalas. In this activity, students gather found materials in nature. They become scavengers, looking for different colors and patterning, or for materials that simply spark their interest. Students have the experience of using their hands in a kinesthetic, somatic, and constructionist way. It is also an ephemeral experience, as the nature mandala is impermanent. Through this activity, students learn that it is not a final product that counts the most, but rather the process and the feelings that move through them during the experience. I introduce students to nature mandalas by showing them examples of the work of Andy Goldsworthy. Students engage in a see–think–wonder activity and are then guided to collect natural materials on their own. This activity can last anywhere from 10 minutes to an hour. It can be done individually or as a group experience. If visiting natural spaces throughout the week is difficult, teachers can bring natural materials inside the classroom. Nature-mandala work can also be incorporated into inquiries into patterning, geometry, and chart- and graph-making in mathematics.

Mindfulness outdoor-education practices help students build and establish a relationship to natural world. They can bring children alive to their feelings and thoughts. The natural world can not only serve as a place to be mindful, but can also serve as a catalyst for creativity.

Senses Cards

hearing

Five senses

taste

sight

smell

hearing

touch

Senses Cards

Senses Cards

Tapping Into Our Senses: K–Grade 2

Page 1

Name: _____   Date: _____

We have five senses. They help us understand the world around us.

1. Touch: We feel things with our fingers and hands and other parts of our bodies.

2. Smell: We smell things with our nose.

3. Taste: We taste things with our tongue. We taste many different flavors.

4. Hearing: We hear sounds with our ears. Some people are not able to hear.

5. Sight: We see things with our eyes. Some people are not able to see.

Pembroke Publishers ©2019 *Fostering Mindfulness* by Shelley Murphy ISBN 978-1-55138-340-8

Tapping Into Our Senses: Grades 3–6

Page 1

Name: _____   Date: _____

Touch: Nerve endings in the parts of the body and in the skin send signals of cold, heat, contact, and pain to the brain. Our skin contains the highest number of nerve endings on our body. People without sight use their sense of touch to read Braille, which is a system of raised dots that are felt with fingertips.

Smell: Our noses have membranes that recognize molecules and send messages to the brain about what we are smelling. We also use our sense of smell to help us taste.

Taste: Our taste buds give us our sense of taste. We are able to taste four different flavors: sweet, salty, bitter, and sour. Everything you taste is one or a combination of these flavors.

Hearing: The outer part of the ear works like a cup or funnel to catch sounds as they travel. For people who are able to hear, vibrations are translated into sounds and are sent for the brain to interpret.

Sight: For people who are able to see, receptor cells tell the brain about the images being perceived. Because eyes bend light, images are actually sent to the brain upside down. The brain eventually turns the image the right way up.

Pembroke Publishers ©2019 *Fostering Mindfulness* by Shelley Murphy ISBN 978-1-55138-340-8

Tapping into Our Senses: All Grades

Page 2

Name: _____   Date: _____

touch

What is one way you used your sense of touch today?

hearing

What did you hear today that you want to remember?

taste

What was the best thing you tasted today?

sight

What did you see today that made you happy?

smell

Describe something that smelled good to you today.

Pembroke Publishers ©2019 *Fostering Mindfulness* by Shelley Murphy ISBN 978-1-55138-340-8

Mystery Sound: K–Grade 2

Name: _____   Date: _____

You are about to play the Mystery Sound Game. If you listen very carefully, it will help you be a better listener. As you listen for the mystery sounds, remember to focus on your breathing. What is the sound you think you hear? Draw or write in the boxes below.

1

2

3

4

5

6

Pembroke Publishers ©2019 *Fostering Mindfulness* by Shelley Murphy ISBN 978-1-55138-340-8

Mindful Mystery Sound : Grades 3–6

Name: _____   Date: _____

You are about to play the Mindful Mystery Sound Game. This game will help you to be a better listener by strengthening your Reticular Activation System (RAS). Remember that this part of you brain can strengthen with practice. As you listen for the mystery sounds, remember to focus on your breathing. What is the sound you think you hear?

1.

2.

3.

4.

5.

6.

Be a Mindful Listener

Name: _____   Date: _____

You just tried a Mindful Listening activity with a partner. Write about your experiences below.

Here is what I liked about being a Mindful Listener:

Here is what was hard about being a Mindful Listener:

Here is what I liked about being the Speaker:

Here is what was hard about being the Speaker:

I preferred being the Mindful Listener.   ☐
I preferred being the Speaker.   ☐

Pembroke Publishers ©2019 *Fostering Mindfulness* by Shelley Murphy ISBN 978-1-55138-340-8

Five-Senses Tour

Name: _____   Date: _____

sight

hearing

touch

taste

smell

In the boxes, write down or draw what you noticed with each of your senses. In the space below, write down what it was like for you to do a mindful sensing tour.

Pembroke Publishers ©2019 *Fostering Mindfulness* by Shelley Murphy ISBN 978-1-55138-340-8

Mindful Eating: Be a Scientist

Name: _____   Date: _____

sight

hearing

touch

taste

smell

In the boxes, write down or draw what you noticed with each of your senses as you eat/ate your food. In the space below, describe what it was like for you to try mindful eating.

Pembroke Publishers ©2019 *Fostering Mindfulness* by Shelley Murphy ISBN 978-1-55138-340-8

5

Mindfulness of Emotions

"We are exploring together. We are cultivating a garden together, backs to the sun. The question is a hoe in our hands and we are digging beneath the hard and crusty surface to the rich humus of our lives."
— Parker J. Palmer

What Is Mindfulness of Emotions?

Mindfulness of one's emotional experiences is central to well-being. Think of your students who are generally good at managing their emotions in positive ways. They are often the same students who show resilience when faced with challenges. The goal of these practices and activities is for students to become skilful at being aware of their emotions as they arise in the present moment and to become familiar with identifying, understanding, using, and managing their emotions in positive ways.

When students are able to identify and manage their own emotions (and those of other people) they are showing what has been called emotional intelligence (Goleman, 1995). Students with strong emotional intelligence are better at managing stress and conflict, showing empathy and kindness, communicating effectively, making informed decisions, building strong relationships, and overcoming challenges. Of course, as teachers know, there is a strong connection between a student's emotions and their behaviors. It is not surprising that research has shown that emotional intelligence is central to success and happiness in life. Studies show that regular mindfulness practice with emotions helps boost emotional intelligence by improving a student's ability to self-regulate in different situations. Regular mindfulness practice helps students become better aware of the connection between their thoughts, emotions, bodily sensations, and behaviors. It helps to create some thoughtful space between a student's actions and reactions. This space strengthens a student's ability to respond more skilfully, instead of letting their feelings and emotional impulses govern their actions.

This is an especially important skill when students are confronted with stressful states and difficult emotions. Mindfulness helps them build emotional awareness, which helps them manage and cope with life's challenges. It also helps them to recognize the emotions of others, which in turn helps them communicate more mindfully and show empathy. While students strengthen their emotional awareness through formal practices, the benefits extend throughout the course of their day, as they become increasingly aware of their emotions and how they influence their behaviors and responses.

Tips for Teaching Mindfulness of Emotions

- Begin with the brain: I like to start mindfulness-of-emotion activities with a brief lesson on mindfulness and its impact on the brain. It gives students an understanding of how their minds work and creates a context for the remaining activities.
- Teach as content: It's helpful to think of emotions and social emotional awareness as content and skills you can teach (explain, model, allow for practice, provide feedback).
- Teach for transfer: The goal is for students to learn about and practice these strategies within the classroom and then use what they have learned in their daily lives.
- Find teachable moments: Find opportunities throughout the day to return to concepts learned; i.e. when students are emotionally reactive, upset, anxious, etc.
- Set boundaries and expectations: In the midst of some of these activities, students may show their vulnerability. It is important to begin these activities with clear expectations about care, compassion, empathy, and respecting the rights and feelings of others.

Mindfulness and the Brain

You can modify this lesson, depending on age and grade level.

I have found when students from Kindergarten on are given the opportunity to learn about how their minds work, they use this knowledge to nurture and strengthen how they regulate their emotional responses, their behaviors, and their attention. This knowledge also helps set the stage for students to understand how mindfulness strengthens their brains, fosters their intellectual and emotional growth, and promotes well-being. This lesson helps ensure students understand the difference between their fight-flight-or-freeze (survival) brain and their prefrontal cortex (learning brain). They also learn how mindfulness helps to support each of these parts of their brains, which ultimately supports self-regulation.

Use scripts as a guide. You may read as-is or modify to fit your needs.

1. You can copy and distribute the Understanding Your Thinking Brain and Survival Brain activity sheet on page 95 or 96 to refer to when talking about parts of the brain with students. You might also wish to search the words *brain* and *amygdala* in Google Images and display the results.
2. Begin the lesson:

   I want to tell you about two very important parts of your brain. One of them is called the survival brain *(the amygdala) and the other is called the* thinking brain *(the prefrontal cortex).*
   Your survival brain (or amygdala) is the oldest, most primitive part of your brain. This part of the brain has been around so long it is sometimes called the reptilian part of the brain. It acts like your own personal bodyguard. Its job is to protect you from threats or danger and to keep you safe, no matter what. It helps you react very quickly and without thinking. Imagine you are standing under a tree and you hear

the sound of a large branch cracking. Your amygdala decides there isn't enough time to think so it turns off your thinking brain (prefrontal cortex) and reacts quickly. It tells your body to move away from under the tree where there is danger. Automatically and without thinking, you quickly move out of the way of the falling branch. Your amygdala bodyguard has done its job. Once you are safe, it allows your thinking brain to go online again.

The problem is, the amygdala can't tell the difference between real or imagined danger, so it makes mistakes. Sometimes when we are stressed, nervous, or angry, our amygdala thinks these are real threats or danger and that it needs to act. For example, if you're stressed because you are about to give a speech in front of the class or you're angry because you just got into an argument with your friend, your amygdala may turn your thinking brain off because it imagines these are real threats or danger. Giving a speech or getting into an argument with a friend may be stressful, but they do not threaten your safety. Remember, the job of the amygdala is to act automatically and without thinking. Sometimes this helps us be safe from danger, but sometimes it causes us to react without thinking.

The prefrontal cortex (or PFC), just above your eyebrows and around your forehead, keeps growing and developing into our 20s. Our PFC or thinking brain helps us plan, pay attention, problem-solve, have self-awareness, and make thoughtful decisions. When you are calm, information flows through the brain and into the PFC so you can make wise choices. But when you are stressed, angry, or upset, your amygdala believes it has to react automatically to save you from danger, so it stops information from getting to your PFC. This would be the right thing for the amygdala to do if you were truly in danger. But when you are not in danger, it makes it a lot harder for you to pay attention, make wise choices, and respond thoughtfully. So you sometimes end up saying or doing things you later regret.

The good news is that, when we practice mindfulness on a regular basis, it helps to make our thinking brain stronger so we can think more clearly, better regulate our emotions and our behavior, and respond more thoughtfully. It also makes the amygdala less reactive when it doesn't need to be.

Just like when people exercise or lift weights to help strengthen their bodies and their muscles, mindfulness practice can help strengthen our brains. Brains grow and change based on how they are used. Have you heard the saying, "Neurons that fire together wire together?" Every time you practice something, neurons in your brain connect. When this happens, your brain grows thicker and stronger in certain places. Mindfulness helps the neurons in your thinking brain connect and grow stronger.

3. You can invite students to complete the Thinking Brain vs Survival Brain activity sheet on page 97 and/or Understanding Your Thinking Brain and Survival Brain activity sheet on page 95 or 96. These activity sheets help students consolidate their learning about the functioning of two key parts of their brains.

Voice from the Classroom: The Amygdala, Prefrontal Cortex, and Hippocampus
by Megann Robert

When I was teaching a Grade 3 homeroom, my students and I went on a journey to learn about the parts of the brain that really affect how we're feeling: the prefrontal cortex, the amygdala, and the hippocampus. We nicknamed them the *control centre*, the *panic centre*, and the *library*.

We talked about how the panic centre helps make sure we stay alive by telling our body to fight, run, or hide, and how important this part of the brain was to early human beings. Then I explained that the library stores memories so it can tell us when we need to be afraid and when we don't need to be afraid. During a conversation with a colleague, she very neatly summarized the concept with a great example: Kindergarteners typically cry during their first fire drill because it's a scary new experience; however, Grade 2 students don't cry because they've experienced fire drills at least four times and their library reminds their control centre that, while it's loud and hectic, nothing bad has ever happened during a drill before.

My students and I devised a T-chart that listed examples of real emergencies that could leave us feeling panicked (e.g., a bear in the school, being lost in a busy place, etc.) and non-emergencies (e.g., not knowing the answer to a question, an upset parent, etc.). Then we made a list of strategies we could use in real emergencies (e.g., call 911, find an adult, etc.) and strategies we could use in non-emergencies (e.g., take a mindful walk down the hallway, get a drink, take some deep breaths, etc.).

From that point on, when a student looked panicked or upset, I would prompt with, "Real emergency or non-emergency?" Each time I prompted with this question, the student would have an *aha!* moment. Students frequently walked over to the strategies chart, asked for permission to do that activity, and then return whenever they were ready. The best part? If I ever looked panicked, one particular student would always prompt me with, "Real emergency or non-emergency?" I couldn't help but smile whenever she asked. I always made it a point to use one of the strategies. After all, we need to practice what we preach!

How Do I Handle This?

When there's **NO** danger, I can...
- use deep breathing
- go for a walk -move
- talk to a trusted person
- listen to music -clean
- focus on something else
- get alone time -get a hug
- meditate -sketch/draw
- journal -have a snack
- get fresh air -nap

EXAMPLES of REAL DANGER!
- Kidnapped · getting lost
- world war · nuclear meltdown
- fighting/wrestling
- being robbed/accosted
- someone following you
- car crash · person w/weapon
- fire at home/school/anywhere
- cutting yourself · sinking boat
- earthquake/tornado

FEELS DANGEROUS, BUT ISN'T!
- Ms. Roberts at a 5
- unfamiliar environment/crowds
- spiders/snakes · taxes (being an adult)
- horror movies/scary music
- angry/upset parents
- going to a new school/high school
- changes in routine
- new job/future · nightmares
- disagreeing with others

Voice from the Classroom: Learning about the Brain
by Vicca Chang, Grade 3 teacher

From day one, when students walk through the door of our third-grade classroom, we talk about the brain. In addition to all the community-building games and activities we do to get to know each other, we also get to know ourselves as learners. We discuss the basic parts and functions of our brains in order to better understand what makes each individual tick. We delve into our emotions, our triggers, and, most importantly, our motivators. Once students are equipped with this knowledge, I believe they become more empowered to take ownership of their learning. Talking about different aspects of the brain lays the foundation for all future lessons, strategies, and exercises when incorporating mindfulness in the classroom.

Our introduction to the brain begins with a read-aloud with a book called *Your Fantastic Elastic Brain* by JoAnn Deak. This book provides a fun and accessible way for children to learn about the parts and functioning of their brains. The students are typically fascinated and, after a lot of questions and a lively discussion, I ask them to get into groups and make a mind map about their learning. We draw the brain in the centre of a big piece of chart paper and, with markers in hand, they map out their ideas using pictures and words. Finally, each individual makes a 3D model of the brain using a template copied onto construction paper. They then write a sentence to describe the name and role of each part of the brain. These brainy works of art are hung from the ceiling and become the centrepiece of our classroom. Students take great pride on Family Welcome Night when they are able to show their loved ones what they know about the brain.

Following the book and 3D model, I try to help students make the connection between what the parts of their brains do and how they self-regulate by showing them Dr Dan Siegel's Hand Model of the Brain (for a quick tutorial, see https://youtu.be/gm9CIJ74Oxw). Children often benefit from a tactile or concrete reference and this model is perfect for helping them visualize something you cannot easily see. I also borrow the language that Dr. Siegel uses to talk to students who are, as he describes, "flipping their lids" when they are in a state of stress. I prompt them to use breathing techniques or other calming activities to self-regulate strong emotions. This year, I found that many of my students were able to use these lessons and strategies to bring themselves back to a calm and present mental state, thereby making our classroom a more peaceful and positive learning environment.

Reaction vs Response

The Mindful Responding activity helps students understand the difference between a reaction and a response. While *reaction* and *response* are terms that are often used interchangeably, they have very distinct meanings.

Reaction

We have all had the experience of saying or doing something "without thinking." It feels like an unconscious and automatic response. This is a reaction. Reactions are often emotional in nature and, more often than not, are influenced by the survival mechanism in our brain (the amygdala), which controls our stress response. In a state of stress, we often do not think clearly and we react.

Response

In contrast, a response is thoughtful and regulated; it is influenced by the conscious mind. During a response, our prefrontal cortex or higher-thinking brain is online. We are aware of our emotions and how they feel in our bodies, and our thinking is clear. In other words, we are mindful in the situation, and this allows us to choose how we respond.

Mindful Responding

When students engage in mindful awareness, it helps them become aware of their emotions before they feel them at their extremes. This helps to create thoughtful space between impulse and action. When students learn to respond to situations rather than react, they are less regretful, they have fewer uncomfortable confrontations and interactions, their social relationships are strengthened, and they have better overall control over their emotional responses and behaviors.

This quick activity teaches students about having a choice in how they respond to their feelings. It also teaches students about options for responding more mindfully and thoughtfully. It helps them develop the tools to be able to express and manage their difficult feelings.

1. Using chart paper, blackboard, or whiteboard, create and write out a few behavior scenarios with the question *Response or Reaction?* at the end of each. Here are a few possible scenarios:

   - I was mad at my friend so I threw something. Response or Reaction?
   - I was jealous so I took some time to think about what I was feeling and why. Response or Reaction?
   - I heard a sudden noise so I screamed. Response or Reaction?
   - Someone hurt my feelings so I took three breaths and then thought about what I would say. Response or Reaction?
   - I was invited to a party so I told my friend I would need to ask my parents first before I could answer. Response or Reaction?

2. Read each scenario out loud or invite students to do so.
3. Ask students to think about whether the people in the scenario have reacted (without thinking) or have responded (mindfully). Ask students to share a rationale for why they think the people in the scenario either reacted or responded.

4. Ask students to Think–Pair–Share a time when they reacted or responded. Remind students that they are not always in control of how they feel but they are in charge of what they do about it.
5. You can invite students to complete the Mindful Responding activity sheet on page 98, to think about ways they can respond more wisely next time they experience a challenging emotion.

Recognizing, Naming, and Managing Emotions

These activities give students opportunities to learn how to recognize, name, and manage their emotions. A landmark study conducted by UCLA Professor of Psychology Matthew D Lieberman and colleagues (2007) found that putting feelings into words makes difficult emotions, such as sadness and anger, less intense. When students learn to notice feelings and put them into words they activate their prefrontal region of the brain (thinking brain), and quiet the amygdala (stress response). In essence, putting feelings into words helps put the brakes on a negative emotional response.

While many students are easily able to identify emotions when they are feeling them at their extreme, they are less able to notice and name them on the way to the extreme. As teachers well know, once students have reached the outburst stage, it's difficult to return. Through mindful emotion practices and activities, students become better attuned to their emotions and behaviors, which leads to a greater likelihood they will be able to regulate them. This can be especially powerful for students with impulse control challenges.

Emotion and Traits Vocabulary Chart

This activity helps students strengthen their vocabularies for identifying/naming and expressing their feelings. It also helps students understand the difference between feelings and traits.

1. You can begin this activity with a read-aloud on the topic of emotions or feelings. I like *In My Heart: A Book of Feelings* by Jo Witek and *My Blue is Happy* by Jessica Young. See Resources section on page 157 for a list of books on feelings)
2. On chart paper or an interactive whiteboard, create a T-Chart with columns marked *Emotions* and *Traits*. Define each term for students: an emotion is a temporary feeling we have in reaction to something; a trait is a part of someone's character or personality (you can sometimes see it in the way they act). Help students understand the difference.
3. Invite students to generate emotion/feeling words. If they offer a word that is a trait and not an emotion, put that word in the trait column and discuss why it is a trait and not a feeling.

Emotions Graffiti Board

Graffiti boards are shared writing spaces where students record their comments, observations, or questions about a topic. These tools give students an opportunity to read and learn about each other's ideas, opinions, and experiences, while incorporating movement and helping create a record of student ideas. It is an inclusive activity in that students—including those who are introverted, anxious, English language learners, less-proficient writers etc.—have an opportunity to share their thoughts without the presenting aspect typically involved in speaking out loud. Students can write or draw responses.

The Emotions Graffiti Board activity gives students practice in thinking about various primary emotions and matching them to their prior experiences. They will read about and learn of others' experiences with emotions, such as joy, fear, anger, and jealousy.

1. On the top of separate pieces of chart paper, write one emotion. Limit the emotions to primary emotions for younger students (e.g., *anger*, *sadness*, *fear*, *joy*, *love*); include a few secondary emotions for older students (e.g., *regret*, *jealousy*, *disappointment*, *guilt*).
2. Place students in groups of three or four. Provide each group with a piece of chart paper labelled with an emotion, large sticky notes. and markers. Students may work at their desks or with chart paper fastened to the wall.
3. Prompt students to look at the emotion on their chart paper and to think about an experience they have had that resulted in this emotion.
4. After allowing for some thinking time, invite each student to write their experience on a large sticky note and place it on their graffiti board. Less-proficient writers can be invited to draw.
5. After 2–3 minutes at one poster board, have groups rotate to the next poster.
6. Repeat the steps until each group has contributed to all graffiti boards.
7. Bring all graffiti boards to the front of the room and work as a class to identify similarities, differences, and patterns.

Emotion Mapping

Emotion mapping gives students an opportunity to take some time to pay attention to how and where they are feeling an emotion, and to give it a name. As we know, when students are able to recognize and name a challenging feeling, it reduces its impact.

See Chapter 8 for more about the Peace Corner.

1. Copy the Emotion Mapping activity sheet on page 99 or 100 and distribute to students to complete at their desks or within the Peace Corner.
2. Invite students to write about or illustrate what they are feeling and where they are feeling it within their bodies. With younger students, let them choose from an illustrated list of primary emotions:

| Excited | Happy | Neutral | Sad | Worried | Angry |

Older students may choose from a more comprehensive list:

Calm	Satisfied	Depressed	Scared
Surprised	Cheerful	Upset	Jealous
Proud	Hopeful	Angry	Uncomfortable
Grateful	Optimistic	Furious	Afraid
Excited	Unhappy	Frustrated	Worried
Wonderful	Hurt	Annoyed	Embarrassed
Happy	Disappointed	Disgusted	Nervous
Joyful	Ashamed	Grumpy	
Glad	Awful	Mad	

Worry Box

My students were aware that I would read the worries placed in the worry box and that I would not share them with anyone unless I thought they might need some help with their worry. Their worries often gave me quite a bit of information about how I could support them academically, socially, and emotionally.

Many students come into our classrooms weighed down by worry. When their brains are stressed and worried, their ability to concentrate is impaired. That is because the reptilian part of the brain (amygdala) interprets the worry as a threat and is consumed with survival. This means there is little room left for thinking and learning. Most often, when children are worried, they are either fixated on an imagined future or on their perception of past events. It can be very uncomfortable to be mentally hijacked this way. One simple yet powerful strategy for helping children deal with their worries is through use of a Worry Box. Students are invited to put their worries in writing (or in images for younger students) and to place them in a container specifically designated for their worries. The simple act of placing their worries in the worry box helps them create some observable distance between themselves and their worries. For many students, it becomes a form of safe containment so they feel settled enough to go back to learning.

1. Decorate a large jar or shoebox with colored paper, ribbons, images, etc. Label the container with the words *Worry Box*.
2. Invite students to write or draw what their worries are.
3. Invite students to place their worries in the box. Just as naming emotions helps students neutralize them, putting their worries in the worry box helps to create a boundary around them. This very act often helps students release their stress and worry.

Gratitude Practice

When I think about gratitude practice, I am reminded of the words of Mr. (Fred) Rogers. He often recounted a story of when he was a young boy and would see scary things on the news:

> My mother would say to me, "Look for the helpers. You will always find people who are helping." To this day, especially in times of disaster, I remember my mother's words and I am always comforted by realizing that there are still so many helpers—so many caring people in the world.

Wise sage that he was, Mr. Rogers was talking about the power of gratitude. He knew what many studies have shown: in general, researchers have found that people who practice gratitude tend to be happier and both physiologically and psychologically healthier, which, in turn, leads to greater resilience. Gratitude has also been shown to increase a sense of connectedness to others, enhance empathy, improve self-esteem, and reduce aggression.

Grateful-Heart Mindfulness

It is largely understood that gratitude is not inherent. Instead, it is something that is cultivated over time as children see peers or adults show gratitude (modelling) and through experience (practice, practice, practice!). Gratitude practice can be as simple as prompting students to think about and record two to three things they are grateful for each day. You may wish to start with a guided gratitude practice for students until they become familiar and comfortable with the concept.

1. Where necessary, help students understand what is meant by gratitude; i.e., feeling thankful.
2. Model expressions of gratitude. Gratitude can be expressed about anything. You might share your gratitude for your morning coffee, for the blue sky, for such a lovely classroom of students, for your family, for your health, for the loyalty of your dog, etc.
3. Students should be seated when you invite them into the practice:

> *Close your eyes or let them get sleepy and let your body relax. Feel the weight of your body on the chair or on the floor and start by noticing three gentle breaths coming into your body and moving out of your body. You might notice your belly or your chest rising and falling as you breathe. Just notice that for a few more breaths.*
> (Pause)
> *We are now going to do a gratitude mindfulness practice. Gratitude is a feeling of being thankful for or appreciative of something or someone. Let's start by thinking of someone you are very grateful for. This could be someone who has taken very good care of you, who has been kind to you, or who has been a good friend to you. Just take a moment to appreciate this person silently.*
> (Pause)
> *Now take some time to think about what else you might be grateful for. It could be something as simple as the sun in the sky, your favorite music, or your strong feet or wheelchair that bring you safely from one place to another. Just take a minute to think about some things you are truly grateful for.*
> (Pause)
> *Now turn your attention back to your breathing. Let's take three mindful breaths. Notice your breath coming into your body and your breath moving out of your body. Breathe in and breathe out until you hear the sound of the bell.*

4. You can invite students to complete the Grateful Heart activity sheet on page 101, to record what they are grateful for.

Gratitude Journal

Once students are comfortable and familiar with a gratitude mindfulness practice, they can be invited to create gratitude journals to write or draw in daily. Gratitude journals are a positive way to start the school day or can be recorded in at any point throughout the day.

1. Prompt students to think of three new people, things, or experiences they are grateful for each time they record in their gratitude journal.
2. See pages 102–103 for Gratitude Journal Cover and Gratitude Journal Page templates. These activity sheets can be used to help you create Gratitude Journals in which students are asked to respond to the following prompts:

When first introducing gratitude practice to your students, you may wish to use the script as a guide. Once students have been introduced to gratitude practice, you can simply invite them to take a moment to think about what they are grateful for and to share or record their responses.

Today I am grateful for…
The best thing about yesterday was…

Gratitude Cards

Once students have had some practice expressing gratitude, it is good to give them an opportunity to act on their gratitude by showing appreciation. Gratitude cards are one way they can do this. I like to start with inviting students to show appreciation for their classmates. It helps build community and foster relationships. Students write private cards to one or more of their classmates to let them know they are appreciated and why. Students are prompted to be specific about what they appreciate about the recipient: e.g., "Thank you for walking to school with me"; "I am grateful you are nice to me"; "Thank you for being a good citizen of our class"; "Thank you for being so funny"; "I am grateful you speak Urdu too."

1. Copy cards from the Gratitude Cards template on page 104 and have them available in a designated area within your class for students to use. For example, gratitude cards can be kept at writing or anchor activity stations, or within the Peace Corner (see Chapter 8) to be filled out when students are inspired throughout the year.
2. Create a gratitude-card mailbox where students can deposit their gratitude cards. Or invite students to deliver their gratitude cards directly to their recipient in the classroom.
3. Gratitude cards can be done as a whole-class activity each month. Students may write gratitude cards to each other or to family members, friends, etc.

Gratitude Tree

In this activity, students are invited to think about and record something they are grateful for on a cut-out of a leaf. Leaves can be printed on green, brown, or any colored paper.

Some students may want to revisit their gratitude journals for reminders. Younger students may wish to draw what they are grateful for, or you might need to scribe what they have shared. Once students have recorded something they are grateful for on their leaf, it can be taped or glued to the branches of a tree outlined on a bulletin board or wall. This will become your Class Gratitude Tree.

It is best to place the first leaves at the top of the trunk and build up and out from there.

1. Using the templates, print and cut out the Gratitude Tree Base Template on page 106 (using brown-colored paper) and enough Gratitude Tree Leaves on page 105 (using a variety of colors) so each student will have at least one leaf.
2. Post chart paper on a bulletin board or on a wall in landscape layout. Tape or glue the Gratitude Tree Base at the bottom of the chart paper.
3. Create a Gratitude Tree Label (*Our Class Gratitude Tree*) to be posted once all the leaves have been added to the gratitude tree.
4. Model by writing one thing (in a word or two) you are grateful for on a leaf to show what completed gratitude leaves will look like. Add your leaf to the tree.
5. Provide each student with one leaf and a marker (have some extra leaves just in case). Ask students to think about one thing they are grateful for and to record this on their leaf.
6. You may ask students to record their one or two words on draft paper in preparation for "publishing" on their leaf to allow for editing feedback.

7. For students who are not able to write, you may scribe for them or invite them to draw.
8. Paste or tape your Gratitude Tree label above the top leaf in your tree.

Loving Kindness

One day many years ago I was travelling across the Golden Gate Bridge in San Francisco. As I reached out my hand to pay the toll at the kiosk, the attendant leaned out of the window, pointed forward, and said, "Your toll has just been paid for by the person in the car in front of you." I turned my head to look forward, but the car was well on its way along the road. I was speechless. I was heartened by such a random act of generosity and kindness, and it had a profound effect on me. It was from that moment I decided I would pay it forward by covering the toll for the person in the car behind me. Each time I have had the opportunity to do this, I experience the same joyful feelings I did when it was first done for me. Such is the power of kindness when it is received and given.

I believe compassion and kindness should be taught as skills, just as we teach other key curriculum content. Neuroscience research has found that our capacity for kindness grows with practice. In other words, it can be strengthened like a muscle. With practice, our compassion circuitry activates the neural network for caring that we share with all mammals. The good news is that it also activates our brain circuits for positive feelings. A daily practice that incorporates kindness and compassion helps to strengthen these circuits.

In his book, *Love and Compassion: Exploring Their Role in Education* (2018), John P. Miller makes the case for cultivating a sense of compassion through something called a Loving Kindness practice. Loving Kindness meditation involves a mental focus on nurturing an attitude of kindness, compassion, care, and love for ourselves and for others. This practice can be done on its own or in combination with other mindfulness practices. Studies show that Loving Kindness meditation not only helps change how we relate to ourselves, it also helps to reduce stress and anxiety, to increase positive emotions and feelings of hope, to foster empathy, and to strengthen intentions of kindness towards and connection with others. One study even showed that Loving Kindness helps to increase grey matter volume in areas of the brain related to emotion regulation (Leung et al, 2013).

A Loving Kindness mindfulness practice typically begins with students sending positive thoughts toward themselves. Next, they move on to sending positive thoughts to someone they care a great deal about, such as a family member or very good friend. Finally, they send positive thoughts to everyone everywhere.

1. Let students know they are going to do a Loving Kindness practice.
2. Invite students into the practice:

> *As you sit comfortably in your chair, imagine there is a string at the top of your head and it is pulling you up just a little bit straighter. Turn your attention to your breathing and notice your belly rising on your in-breath and falling on your out-breath.*
>
> (Pause)
>
> *We are now going to do a Loving Kindness practice. Once you get comfortable and familiar with this practice, you'll be able to try this on your own. The purpose is to send positive thoughts to yourself and others. Doing this practice helps us to be kinder and more compassionate toward ourselves and others. We'll begin by sending positive*

thoughts to ourselves, and then move on to sending them to someone we care about, and finally to sending them to all beings everywhere. Listen and imagine these words in your mind as I say them.

May I be healthy, happy, and strong.
May I be cared for and loved.
May I be safe and at peace.

May you be healthy, happy, and strong.
May you be cared for and loved.
May you be safe and at peace.

May all beings everywhere be healthy, happy, and strong.
May all beings everywhere be cared for and loved.
May all beings everywhere be safe and at peace.

For variations on this practice and for a more in-depth understanding, see a wonderful book called *Loving-Kindness: The Revolutionary Art of Happiness* by Sharon Salzberg. I recommend it highly.

Voice from the Classroom: Self-Regulation Anchor Chart
by Maddie Cumbaa

One of the greatest joys and challenges of teaching in Early Years is guiding our students to understand and manage their emotions in a healthy way. We know children have complex emotional experiences but, at such a young age, they are often unsure how to recognize warning signs of distress, or how to get back in control of their emotions once they become overwhelmed. How many times have we all dealt with a child's outburst of tears (or fists!) when a situation doesn't go as planned, or a child acting out in class, unable to refocus after a conflict with a friend at recess? An episode like this can derail a child's whole day and make it much harder for them to get back into a learning mindset. Since I have incorporated mindfulness-based practices in my classroom, I have noticed a significant increase in my students' ability to self-regulate when encountering difficulties, which has resulted in a calmer and more cohesive classroom community.

One of the most powerful tools I have encountered for developing emotional awareness in early years learners is a simple anchor chart. Instead of math concepts or success criteria, this anchor chart contains suggestions for ways children can self-regulate in times of stress or upset. I introduce the anchor chart like I would any other; I show the children the chart and read through each of the options on it. We then practice each of the options as a group and discuss in which situations they might be useful. I post the anchor chart at eye-level and refer to it over the course of the year when discussing emotional awareness or unpacking a situation with the children.

The specific options on the chart change depending on my classroom set-up and the group of students I have that year. Generally, I try to include at least one sensory experience (hugging a special stuffed toy), one physical experience (doing a lap of the hallway), one redirection activity (practicing skip-counting or making a list of rhyming words), one comfort experience (looking at a picture the child has drawn of their safe space), and one meditative experience (mindful breathing). Each student tends to gravitate toward one strategy in particular; the most common is mindful breathing.

Many of my students use mindful breathing to self-regulate when they are feeling agitated; a few moments of deep breaths allows them to de-escalate and find their calm again. Earlier this year, for example, I asked my students to complete a mind map as an assessment of their learning in our most recent math unit. Alex, one of my more anxious students, kept coming up to me to ask questions. I would answer and Alex would return to her mind map. However, before her pencil even touched her paper again, she was back up and asking me something else. I could sense she was getting stressed, so I took her aside to check in. "Alex," I said, "is everything okay?" She nodded, but I noticed tears in her eyes. "It seems to me that you're feeling upset. Is that the case?" Alex nodded, explaining, "I know that I know the answers, but can't find them in my head. I don't like making mistakes." I reassured her, reminding her that the most important thing was to try her best and that it wasn't about getting everything correct. I then suggested she use the anchor chart and pick a strategy to help her work through her emotions. Alex walked over to the chart, read through it, and came back to let me know that she wanted to do some mindful breathing. She then walked over to our Quiet Carpet, sat down, and closed her eyes.

Alex placed her hands on her belly, as we had practiced, and I watched as she became more still and her shoulders relaxed. After a few minutes, Alex opened her eyes, stood up, and walked back to my desk asking, "Can I flip my page over and start again?" I happily agreed and Alex soon completed the majority of the mind map. When we debriefed afterwards, Alex explained to me that she had picked mindful breathing because it helps her "find space in her brain" to think of things other than her anxiety. While Alex, and my other students, have learned a variety of support strategies over the course of the year, Alex was not able to remember these strategies in the midst of her anxiety. Having the anchor chart available gave her a visual cue for ways she could get back to a place of calm.

It has been incredibly fulfilling to watch my students learn to use the anchor chart and take ownership of their mental health. Whether they choose mindful breathing, a walk, chair yoga, or any of the other strategies available, the children are developing an understanding of how emotions can affect them mentally and physically and how they can use this emotional awareness to avoid or lessen the impact of being overwhelmed. Having a visual reminder of different self-regulation strategies ensures that my students can attempt to manage their emotions independently, even when they may be too agitated to remember what to do on their own. These small children, after all, have big emotions. A simple anchor chart can help them find their way back to being calm.

Understanding Your Thinking and Survival Brain:
K– Grade 2

Name: _____ Date: _____

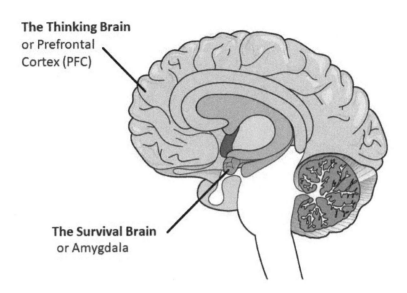

The Thinking Brain
or Prefrontal
Cortex (PFC)

The Survival Brain
or Amygdala

Draw a line to connect each part of the brain with its definition:

Definition:

When we are calm, this part of
our brain helps us **think clearly**
and make **wise decisions**

This part of our brain acts like our
own personal bodyguard. Its job
is to **protect us** from threats or
danger. It **reacts very quickly** and
without thinking.

Part of the Brain:

Prefrontal Cortex (Thinking Brain)

Amygdala (Survival Brain)

Adapted from *The MindUP Curriculum Grades 3–5: Brain-Focused Strategies for Learning-and Living.* New York: Scholastic Teaching Resources.

Pembroke Publishers ©2019 *Fostering Mindfulness* by Shelley Murphy ISBN 978-1-55138-340-8

Understanding Your Thinking and Survival Brain: Grades 3–6

Name: _____   Date: _____

Label these parts of your brain. In the boxes below, describe what their function is.

The Amygdala

```



```

The Prefrontal Cortex

```



```

Adapted from *The MindUP Curriculum Grades 3–5: Brain-Focused Strategies for Learning-and Living.* New York: Scholastic Teaching Resources.

Thinking Brain vs Survival Brain

Name: _____   Date: _____

Now that you've learned about your Thinking Brain (Prefrontal Cortex) and your Survival Brain (Amygdala), decide which brain is being used in the following scenarios:

1. I saw a snake on the sidewalk and I jumped to the side.

   This was my _____ brain in action.

2. My friend said something I didn't like, so I took 3 deep breaths and then responded.

   This was my _____ brain in action.

3. I was angry so I threw my book on the ground.

   This was my _____ brain in action.

4. I got mad at carpet time so I went into the Peace Corner to calm down.

   This was my _____ brain in action.

6. A basketball was coming toward my head and I ducked out of the way.

   This was my _____ brain in action.

7. I had to give a speech in front of the class so I did five-finger breathing so I would be less nervous.

   This was my _____ brain in action.

Mindful Responding

Name: _____   Date: _____

You can't always control your emotions or how you feel, but you can control how you respond. When you practice mindfulness, you learn how to respond to your emotions more thoughtfully and wisely. Think about how you can respond more wisely the next time you experience a challenging emotion.

When I get into an argument with someone and I feel angry I can _____
_____

When I feel sad about something I can _____
_____

When I feel worried about something in the future I can _____
_____

When I feel disappointed that something didn't work out I can _____
_____

When I feel frustrated that something isn't going my way I can _____
_____

When I feel jealous I can _____
_____

When I feel scared I can _____
_____

Pembroke Publishers ©2019 *Fostering Mindfulness* by Shelley Murphy ISBN 978-1-55138-340-8

Emotion Mapping: K–Grade 2

Name: _____   Date: _____

Circle or color the emotion that best matches how you are feeling right now.

It helps to name the emotion we are feeling. Circle the word that best matches how you are feeling:

Excited   Happy   Neutral   Sad   Worried   Angry

Take three mindful breaths and listen to your body. Where do you feel this emotion? Does your emotion have a color? With a colored pencil, mark where you feel it most and write about what you are feeling.

_____

_____

_____

_____

_____

If you are having a difficult emotion, think of something you can do to help yourself feel better (Five-Finger Breathing, Mindful Coloring, Mindful Movement, etc.). What will you try?

Emotion Mapping: Grades 3–6

Name: _____   Date: _____

When we learn to name the emotions we are feeling, it helps us to manage them better. We make wiser choices and feel happier. Can you find the words to describe what you are feeling right now?

Calm	Satisfied	Depressed	Scared
Surprised	Cheerful	Upset	Jealous
Proud	Hopeful	Angry	Uncomfortable
Grateful	Optimistic	Furious	Afraid
Excited	Unhappy	Frustrated	Worried
Wonderful	Hurt	Annoyed	Embarrassed
Happy	Disappointed	Disgusted	Nervous
Joyful	Ashamed	Grumpy	
Glad	Awful	Mad	

Take three mindful breaths and tune into your body more closely. Where in your body do you feel this emotion? On the image below, mark where you feel it most. Use the lines to write about what you are feeling and why.

_____

_____

_____

_____

_____

If you are having a difficult emotion, think of something you can do to help yourself feel better (Five-Finger Breathing, Mindful Coloring, Mindful Movement, etc.). What will you try?

Pembroke Publishers ©2019 *Fostering Mindfulness* by Shelley Murphy ISBN 978-1-55138-340-8

Grateful Heart

Name: _____   Date: _____

You just did a gratitude mindfulness practice. Remember, gratitude is a feeling of being thankful for something or someone. Use the space below to write or draw what you are grateful for.

I am grateful for

I am grateful for

Gratitude Journal Cover

My
Gratitude
Journal

This Gratitude Journal belongs to

_____

Pembroke Publishers ©2019 *Fostering Mindfulness* by Shelley Murphy ISBN 978-1-55138-340-8

Gratitude Journal Page

Gratitude Journal

Date: _____ _____

Today I am grateful for...

The best thing about yesterday was...

Gratitude Cards

Pembroke Publishers ©2019 *Fostering Mindfulness* by Shelley Murphy ISBN 978-1-55138-340-8

Gratitude Tree Leaf

Gratitude Tree Base

6

Mindful Movement

What Is Mindful Movement?

Mindful movement is an active mindfulness practice that invites students to move their bodies in a thoughtful and focused way while, at times, being attentive to their micro-movements. It is a way to help students bring awareness to the connection between their bodies and minds through focused attention and a repeated linking of their movements with their breath. Using physical movement as an entry point for mindfulness practice is not new. Mindful movement, in the form of yoga and tai chi, has been around for centuries. Research links this type of mindful movement to improvements in self-awareness, balance and coordination, behavior control, and cognition. It also helps to activate the parasympathetic nervous system, which helps to induce a calm state.

Studies show that when students are given an opportunity to direct their awareness toward intentional movements and to continually shift their attention as they move, they not only improve their ability to focus their attention but also transfer this type of cognitive control to other tasks at hand throughout the school day and beyond (Zelazo and Lyons, 2012). This is helpful for all students, particularly for students who typically have a difficult time controlling their attention. A study from NYU published in the *American Journal of Occupational Therapy* (2015) found that mindful yoga exercises improved strength, motor coordination, social skills, concentration, and focus in children with autism spectrum disorders.

Tips for Teaching Mindful Movement

- Mindful movement activities can be integrated into the schedule at any point throughout the class/day.
- Mindful movement activities are especially helpful before a transition or as a break from activities that require sustained attention.

- Activities can be modified, shortened, or lengthened as appropriate to grade level.
- Each student's body has its own physical strengths and challenges. Mindful movement exercises can be easily adapted to suit individual student needs.
- For most mindful movement exercises, it is helpful to model for students before asking them to attempt for the first time.

Mindful Heartbeat

Use scripts as a guide. You may read as-is or modify to fit your needs.

This is an excellent introductory mindful movement activity that invites students to become aware of their bodies and to connect to the present through their heartbeats. They will become aware of their heartbeats both before and after a brief movement exercise. Students who are able to stand/jump can do jumping jacks; students who need to remain seated can do the arm movements.

1. Have a timer ready.
2. Invite students into the practice:

   Today you are going to try something called the Mindful Heartbeat activity. In this activity, you're going to pay careful attention to your heartbeat and your breathing before you move and after you move. Now, everyone raise your right hand in the air. Your right hand is going to help you pay mindful attention to your heartbeat and your breathing. Now take your mindful hand and place it over your heart like this.
   (Model for students)
   If you're comfortable with it, close your eyes or let your eyes get sleepy. Bring mindfulness awareness to your heartbeat. Pay attention to what you notice. Can you feel it pump in your chest? If you don't notice anything, that's okay. Sometimes our hearts are very quiet as they are doing their jobs.
   (Pause)
   What do you notice about your breathing? Is it fast or slow?
   (Pause)
   Would anyone like to share what you noticed about your heartbeat or your breathing?
   (Invite responses. You may wish to record these on chart paper, whiteboard, etc.)

3. Continue lesson:

   Now we are going to move. You are going to do 20 jumping jacks (or arm jacks) or as many as you can.
   (Circulate as students move; movement should last about 15 seconds)

4. Continue lesson:

   Now that you are standing or sitting still, go ahead and raise your mindful hand and place it on your heart again.
   (Model for students)
   Close your eyes and let your eyes get sleepy. Bring careful awareness to what you notice. What do you feel against your hand? Can you feel your heart pumping in your chest? Is your heart pumping fast or slow? How does it feel against your hand? What do you notice about your breathing? Is your chest or belly rising and falling quickly or slowly? Keep your eyes closed and spend the next minute or so keeping your awareness on your heartbeat and your breathing. Do this until you hear the sound of the bell.

5. You can invite students to complete the Mindful Heartbeat activity sheet on page 116, to record what they noticed about their heartbeat and their breathing before and after they exercised their bodies.

Mindful Mirroring

For younger students, you may want to introduce this exercise sitting down, with you as the leader and the rest of the class as the mirrors. Once students become familiar and comfortable with the exercise, they can move into partners.

This activity is a fun and engaging mindful movement exercise that invites students to mirror each other's movements. It helps students to become aware of their own bodies and to build their awareness of others around them. In building this awareness, it can also be powerful in cultivating and strengthening relationships within the classroom. The goal of the exercise is to practice mindful movement and mirroring in a way that makes it difficult for an observer to figure out who is leading and who is mirroring.

1. Get students into partners and ask them to sit or stand facing each other about a metre apart.
2. Model mindful mirroring with one of your students, showing how slow and deliberate movements should be.
3. Begin the modelling:

You are now about to do a mindful mirroring activity with your partner. One of you will start by being the leader *and the other will be the* mirror. *You will have a chance later to switch roles. Decide who will be the leader first. If you can't decide, the leader will be the person whose name starts with the letter that comes first in the alphabet.*

All leaders, please raise your hands. Your job will be to face your partner, look into their eyes or face and move your arms and hands. Move them very mindfully and slowly, bringing awareness to each of your movements. Make sure it's easy for your partner to mirror your movements. You are not trying to trick your partner. Your job is to make it easy for them to match or mirror your movements.

Now, raise your hand if you are the mirror. Your job will be to look into your partner's eyes or face and follow their movements exactly. At first, you might want to move your eyes to watch your partner's hands and arms as they move. It's important that you keep looking at your partner's face so it continues to look like a mirror.

Remember, while there is a lot of slow, mindful movement during this activity, there is no talking. Imagine someone is watching you and your partner do this mindful mirroring activity. Your goal is to make it hard for them to be able to figure out who is the leader and who is the mirror. Are there any questions?

Okay, leaders, you may begin leading. Mirrors, you may begin mirroring. I'll ring the bell in about a minute when it's time to switch.

As they become more proficient with this activity, they will be able to switch their roles in mid-movement.

4. Ring the bell to switch roles after one minute.
5. You might select a pair of students you notice were doing a particularly good job of Mindful Mirroring; i.e., it was difficult for you to tell who was leading and who was mirroring. Invite this pair to do Mindful Mirroring for the class. Have the class guess who is mirroring and who is leading.
6. You can have students Think–Pair–Share and/or share as a whole class what it was like to practice Mindful Mirroring.
7. You can invite students to write about what it was like to be in the Mindful Leader role and the Mindful Mirror role.

Mindful Walking

Walking becomes a mindfulness practice when we consciously focus our attention on the micro movements of our bodies as we move one leg in front of the other. When first introducing mindful walking to students, it's helpful to model and then guide them along with your instruction. As mindful walking becomes more familiar, they will learn to practice on their own. They may also practice mindful walking with a partner; i.e., one person leads while the other follows behind and walks in sync. A student who uses a wheelchair may focus on their arm or hand movements as they move their chair.

1. Invite students to stand up. If possible, have them form a large circle around the periphery of the classroom. Students need just enough space to walk slowly and mindfully in one direction without bumping into other students.
2. Invite students into the practice:

> *Let your body get comfortable as you stand in place. Turn your awareness to your shoulders and let them drop. Now imagine there is a string at the top of your head and it's pulling your whole body up a little straighter. Both feet are touching the ground and your hands are at your sides.*
>
> *You are now going to try something called Mindful Walking. Walking is something most of us do every single day without thinking about it. Today, you're going to think about it as you walk mindfully. Remember when we are mindful, it means that we are paying attention to what's happening right now. Sometimes we use an anchor to remind us to come back to the present. In this mindfulness practice, you are letting your feet be your anchor. Now, with your eyes looking down at your feet begin to walk slowly—very slowly. Pay careful attention to the feeling in each part of your feet as they lift off of the ground and then touch the ground as you move. Notice when your heel touches the ground and your toes follow. Notice when the heel of your other foot begins to lift off of the ground to move forward. Just stay with the sensations of parts of your feet touching the ground and then lifting as you move.*
>
> *When you are no longer focusing on your feet touching the ground, this means your mind has wandered. That's okay. Just bring your awareness back to the feeling of your feet slowly moving on the ground and keep your attention/awareness here until you hear the sound of the bell and it recedes.*

3. Invite students to return to their seats.
4. You can have students Think–Pair–Share their experiences of Mindful Walking.

Mindful Yoga Movement

On page 121, you will find a Mindful Yoga Response activity sheet. This is optional and can be used for students to record what it was like for them to try Mindful Yoga poses and how their body and mind felt as they tried it.

Mindful yoga gives students an opportunity to incorporate slow, deliberate movements while focusing the mind and connecting to the body. This section on Mindful Yoga Movement was written by Carrie Poteck, who has conducted research on improving student well-being through mindfulness.

See pages 117–120 for Yoga Pose Cards with images of each of the Yoga poses. These can be used in a pocket chart or displayed for the class to view when leading small groups or the whole class through yoga poses. They can also be placed at stations, in the Peace Corner (see Chapter 8), or at individual or clustered desks as a visual way to remind students of mindful movement strategies they can use to self-regulate. The cards are ready to run on heavy paper, such as cardstock and can be laminated.

Plow pose

Boat pose

Teaching Mindful Yoga Movement

by Carrie Poteck, Teacher and Internationally Certified Yoga Instructor

Yoga is a time for enjoyment, when students can gain a deeper sense of connection between their body and mind. Yoga can be used as a tool for exploratory fun and to expand self-awareness. Students gain insight on their thought patterning, such as where their minds go when they wander. Yoga also strengthens their attention by keeping a sustained level of focus on their body movements. This means that they are incorporating the element of mindfulness by focusing their attention on each movement and each breath throughout the practice.

Please remind your class that they should listen to their bodies. This means letting them know that if something feels uncomfortable they should not force themselves into a pose. Everyone's body is different, which means the pose will look different for everyone, and that is okay. This means that students should not compare the way their pose looks with anyone else's pose.

Feel free to turn off the lights and remove distractions. You may want to turn on calming or relaxing music (preferably with no words). Yoga should be practiced with grace, ease, no judgment, and a light-hearted nature that welcomes laughter. You may do one or several poses in a row. Do whatever works for your students and your classroom setting. Have fun!

Plow Pose

Lying on your back, bend your knees and put the bottom of your feet on the ground. Put your hands on your lower back and lift one foot and then the other up toward the sky. Reach your feet up high as your back peels off the ground. Keep your head still, chest coming close to your chin. You can keep your legs straight up here, or go deeper by bringing your feet over your body, reaching toward the ground behind your head. Do not move your head side to side. Breathe deeply here feeling your spine stretching.
(Stay here for approximately five deep breaths).
To come out of the pose, use your hands to hold your back and slowly roll down until you're flat on your back.

Boat Pose

Sit on your bottom with your knees bent and your feet on the floor in front of you. Lean your upper body back just a little bit and lift your feet off of the floor until they're in line with your knees. You can keep your knees bent or straighten your legs up to the sky; straightened legs would make your body shape look like the letter V. You can keep your hands on the floor, holding the back of your thighs, or reach them forward toward your knees (so arms are parallel to the ground). Pull your belly in toward your spine to keep your body strong! Make sure your back is straight, not curved, and your shoulders are relaxed away from your ears. Remember not to hold your breath! To release this pose, bring your hands back beside your body and place your feet back on the ground. Take a few breaths.

Tree pose

Triangle pose

Belly breathing

Tree Pose

Standing with both feet apart, lift up your toes, spread them out, and place them back down. Bring a little bend to your knees so your knee joint isn't locked. Stand on the left foot and gently lift the right foot off of the ground. Stare at one spot on the ground in front of you to help you balance. Open the right knee and hip toward the right side of the room and place the bottom of your right foot on your left leg. Make sure the foot is above or below your knee (not on the knee). Bring your palms to your heart centre or reach your hands up to the sky. Feel your body growing tall; breathe deeply with your back straight. Make sure you're breathing all the way down to your belly. It's okay to feel your body swaying around—just like how a tree blows in the wind. Imagine your left foot has roots moving into the earth. To come out of the pose, bring your hands down beside your body, bring your knee forward, and place your foot back on the earth. Shake and wiggle the body to release the pose. Repeat on the other leg.

Triangle Pose

Stand with your feet very wide apart (about one metre). Turn your left foot to the side (so it is perpendicular to the right foot). Lift your arms up so they're in line with your shoulders, palms facing the wall in front of your body, head looking toward your left hand. Push your hips to the right and reach your torso and left arm toward your left foot. Bring your left hand down toward the ground and right hand up toward the sky. Look at your right thumb. Breathe in. Make sure your knees have a little bend and aren't locked. Breathe in, feeling your spine nice and straight. To come out of the pose, slowly lift your body back up and step your feet together. Repeat on the other side.

Belly Breathing

Sit in a comfortable position (legs crossed or sitting on your knees). Place both hands on your belly. Inhale slowly and feel your belly grow bigger.
(Pause)
Exhale slowly, feeling your belly shrink and your body relax.
(Pause)
Inhale, keeping your shoulders and face relaxed. Exhale and let the air move out of your body slowly and softly. Try to focus on taking a deep in-breath. On the out-breath, let every last bit of air leave your body. Inhale, expand. Exhale, release.
(Repeat script as many times as you like and let the pace of your voice get slower and slower as you progress.)

Warrior pose

Down dog pose

Warrior Pose

Stand with your feet hip-distance apart. Take a big step back with your right foot and turn it toward one o'clock. Bend your left leg and keep your right leg long and straight. When you look down at your left knee, you should still be able to see your left toes. Make sure your hips are both facing forward. Don't let the right hip get pulled back with your right foot! Keeping your back straight (no arch in your spine), take a breath in and reach your arms up to the sky. As you exhale, think of your shoulders moving down your back and away from your ears. Imagine you have a big beach ball between your hands that you're holding onto very strongly. Feel the warrior strength running through your body as your feet are pushing into the earth and the strength runs all the way up to your fingertips. Breathe here (for as many breaths as you'd like to hold the pose). To come out of the pose, bring your hands to your heart centre, palms touching, and step your right foot back beside your left foot.

Down Dog Pose

Start on your hands and knees. Measure the size of two fists between your knees to make sure they're the perfect distance apart. Place hands on the earth and spread your fingers wide apart. Pull your belly in, lift your knees off the ground, and reach your bottom up toward the sky. Your body will look like an upside down letter V. Knees can stay a little bit bent. Feel your chest moving closer to your legs while your spine is very straight. Keep reaching your bottom up to the sky and feel your heels getting closer to the earth. Your eyes are looking at your belly button; the back of your neck is in line with the rest of the spine. Feel your breath moving through your body. To release this pose, bend your knees and place them on the ground. Sink your bottom back to your heels and reach your arms forward. Place your forehead on the earth. Take a nice deep breath.

Voice from the Classroom: Mindful Movement
by Carrie Poteck

I currently teach a very high-energy group of 25 sixth-grade students. As it happens, most of them are boys. I began teaching this class mid-year and self-regulation has been our largest area of focus. My class has a diverse range of needs, including three students identified with ADHD, one student with ASD, and a number of others who have behavioral needs and learning disabilities. Many students have stressful home lives and school is their place of refuge. I believe that what is holding this group back from being their happiest, most-resilient selves and learning to the best of their potential is their underdeveloped ability to empathize and self-regulate. Despite hearing from other teachers about many of my students' erratic behaviors, I found myself shocked during my first week of teaching them. After recess, many students would enter the class turbulently and crowd around to inform me of verbal or physical conflicts, or they would act noticeably upset. Other students would enter with extremely high energy and have difficulty sitting still or calming down. Diving right into a math lesson was counterintuitive, as their focus was not where it could be. Often during lessons there was constant chatter, shouting out of answers, and off-topic and disrespectful comments made amongst the students and even to staff members. I immediately knew that this class would greatly benefit from a mindfulness practice.

I believe that mindful movement works well with this group and other children because they are able to connect to their physical bodies and breath, which is often very difficult for many them. How can you expect someone to be still when they don't recognize that they're moving in the first place? A few minutes of mindful breathing with gentle movement is a useful way for students to self-reflect and become aware of more than just their breath. They are also able to tap into an awareness of their thought patterns.

From short, shallow breathing (which happens after lots of fast/unconscious movement or conflict) I guide them into long, slow belly breaths. We often do this standing before coming down to a seated, mindful movement in their chairs. The body movement alongside the deeper breathing evokes a parasympathetic nervous system response. This helps slow down their racing minds. They must be completely attentive to the sound of my voice as I move from one movement to the next. I make sure to talk in a very quiet voice, almost a whisper; if they talk over me or let distractions take over, they will miss what I say.

Sometimes the movements will be as simple as head turns coordinated with breath, shoulder rolls, leaning forward to touch their toes, or standing back upon their inhalation. These are simple movements but, led almost in slow motion, are more challenging than they expect! I always guide them on inhalations and exhalations, as well as physical cues on where each part of their body should be: for example, "Shoulders soft, face relaxed; inhale as you turn your head to the left; hold it here and exhale very slowly; pause; inhale your head back to centre; exhale while observing your spine—is it long and upright?" I tend to overemphasize the transitions from one movement to the next and make breath awareness an integral part of the practice. We may spend a few minutes moving from one pose to another, with many different cues on how each part of the body is involved in each pose.

It is important to note that I incorporate a lot of background education across all subject areas on what self-regulation is (shared readings in literacy), the effects mindfulness can have on people (health curriculum), the body's fight-or-flight response (science curriculum), how to show yourself and others compassion (drama skits), thought-pattern check-ins, mental awareness of one's thoughts, breath observation, and the effect that mindful movement can have holistically on one's body. To get students to buy in when I first introduce these practices, I use celebrity endorsements from YouTube or quotes and interviews from sports players, actors/actresses, and other celebrities. This helps persuade them mindfulness is something worthwhile and it normalizes the practice.

Fast forward four months: this group of students has an established mindfulness practice and there are huge improvements all around. They report an increase in happiness and lower stress; I see more empathetic behaviors and an increase in focus and attention span. Overall, the students treat themselves, each other, and me more respectfully. Although we now employ many different mindfulness practices, mindful movement is the one that they enjoy the most.

Mindful Heartbeat

Name: _____   Date: _____

You just tried the Mindful Heartbeat activity. You probably noticed there was a difference in how you felt before and after. Use the space below to describe what you noticed.

What did you notice about your heartbeat and your breathing before you exercised your body?

What did you notice about your heartbeat and your breathing after you exercised your body?

Pembroke Publishers ©2019 *Fostering Mindfulness* by Shelley Murphy ISBN 978-1-55138-340-8

Yoga Pose Cards

Plow pose

Boat pose

Pembroke Publishers ©2019 *Fostering Mindfulness* by Shelley Murphy ISBN 978-1-55138-340-8

Yoga Pose Cards

Triangle pose

Tree pose

Yoga Pose Cards

Belly breathing

Warrior pose

Yoga Pose Cards

Down dog pose

Pembroke Publishers ©2019 *Fostering Mindfulness* by Shelley Murphy ISBN 978-1-55138-340-8

Mindful Yoga Response

Name: _____   Date: _____

Mindful Yoga gives you a chance to be thoughtful about the way you move. What was it like for you to try mindful yoga poses? Which yoga pose was your favorite? Choose one yoga pose and describe how your body and your mind felt as you tried it.

Plow pose   Boat pose   Tree pose   Triangle pose   Belly breathing   Warrior pose   Down dog pose

7

Guided Mindfulness

"What do you plan to do with this one wild and precious life?"
— Mary Oliver

What Is Guided Mindfulness?

These practices and activities are a way to guide students through mindfulness as they use visualization, awareness of body sensations, or their imagination as an anchor. The goal is for students to maintain their awareness in every moment through guided mindfulness or imagery. Students are prompted to notice when their mind has wandered and to come back to listening to your voice (live or recorded) as they continue to be guided. Students may notice experiences such as distraction, boredom, frustration, or relaxation. All of these are expected. The goal is for students to notice these experiences as they arise and to bring mindful awareness to listening to your voice and noticing their experience. As we have seen in previous chapters, when we give students opportunities to practice focusing their attention on something (i.e., their breath, their senses, movement etc.) they strengthen their capacity to choose what they pay attention to. A student's ability to pay attention is further strengthened when they are asked to purposefully switch their attention from one thing to another. It helps to build their "attention muscle" and the part of the brain that helps them be less reactive and more present. It is much like building a bicep through resistance training with a weight. Brain science also recognizes the phenomenon of brain plasticity and the power of repeated guided practice.

A slight variation of guided mindfulness is guided imagery. Guided imagery is a meditative practice that uses visualization and imagination to bring awareness to the mind–body connection. Guided imagery invites students to use their imaginations to create mental images that tap into their sensory perception of sights, sounds, smells, movement, textures, etc. Research shows that, because it encourages the brain to imagine positive experiences, guided imagery helps create and strengthen neural pathways for feeling good and calm, and for developing healthy coping skills, new behaviors, and learning. Guided imagery has also been shown to enhance self-esteem, creativity, and positive behaviors while also helping with test anxiety and social stress. Brain studies show guided imagery can help contract muscles, even when they are not actually contracting in real time; when we have thoughts of exercise, our muscles are tricked into micro-contractions as though they are actually doing the exercise. Perhaps it is no surprise that Olympic athletes are among those who routinely use guided imagery techniques to improve their mental and physical performance.

Tips for Teaching Guided Mindfulness

- This type of mindfulness practice is often guided by a script read by the teacher or listened to from a recording.
- When reading from a script or recording your voice, be sure to pace your reading so it is experienced as relaxing and includes appropriate pauses.
- Students can do these exercises when sitting in their chairs or lying on the floor.
- It is not uncommon for students' minds to wander during guided mindfulness practices, particularly at first. Simply remind them this is expected and is a part of the practice.
- Prompt students to imagine they are inside of a story unfolding/playing like a movie in their minds; just as when they are watching a movie, they may get distracted, but will continue to bring their attention back to the film.
- While relaxation is often a by-product of guided mindfulness or mindfulness with guided imagery, the ultimate goal is to give students an opportunity to anchor themselves in the present moment and away from busy and chattering minds.
- I have recorded mindfulness stories for students to listen to when they are on their own, either at home or in class (e.g., in the Peace Corner). The recordings can also be played when you are absent. They can be a great help to students who tend to be more dysregulated in your absence.

Introduction to Guided Practice

Use scripts as a guide. You may read as-is or modify to fit your needs.

In this introductory exercise, students are simply instructed to use their imaginations to become aware of a series or sequence of objects as they are guided by your voice. You should not pause for long between naming a series of objects. The goal is for students to be able to imagine an object in their mind and then to switch their attention swiftly. This helps to sharpen their concentration skills. It is an opportunity for them to practice detached awareness and to let the objects, like thoughts, come and go.

1. Create a list of simple objects you believe students are familiar with; e.g., blue sky, a spider web, an ice cream cone, etc.
2. Students should be sitting for this activity.
3. Invite students into the practice:

   In this mindfulness exercise, you will keep your eyes closed and listen to my voice as I name some objects. I'll start by naming an object and you'll imagine it in your mind. Soon, I'll name another object and you'll shift your attention to imagining this. You'll spend just a few seconds becoming aware of each object in your mind. Imagine you are visualizing each object appearing on and then moving off a digital screen.

Because you are moving your attention from one thing to another on purpose, this exercise is helping you to strengthen your concentration skills.

If you notice you are no longer listening to my voice or visualizing the object, it means you have become distracted. That's okay. Just bring your attention back to imagining your object and listening to my voice.

Let's start by closing your eyes or letting them get sleepy. Place a hand on your belly and take three mindful breaths. Breathe in through your nose and out through your mouth.

(Pause)

Notice how this feels in your body and how your hand rises when you breathe in and falls when you breathe out. Just notice your belly and ride the waves of your breathing.

(Pause)

Now, use your mind to imagine this series of objects. Remember to switch your attention when you hear me name a new object. Start by noticing a cat;

(Count of five)

clouds in the sky;

(Count of five)

a fish swimming in water;

(Count of five)

a pink flower;

(Count of five)

a spider web;

(Count of five)

a water slide;

(Count of five)

a small dog running across a green field;

(Count of five)

trees blowing in the wind;

(Count of five)

an ice-cream cone;

(Count of five)

a giraffe;

(Count of five)

a young child smiling;

(Count of five)

the sun shining.

(Count of five)

Now, turn your attention back to your breathing. Noticing the rise and fall of your belly as you breathe in and breathe out. Keep your awareness on your breath until you hear the sound of the bell.

3. Ask students to consider and then share in partners or as a whole class what it was like for them to shift their imagination and attention from one object to another.

Body Scan

The body scan exercise is a way to guide our students' awareness to each part of their bodies in a sequential and structured way. It is considered a foundational

I like to use a count of five in between naming each object.

mindfulness practice (Kabat-Zinn, 1990) that provides an opportunity to strengthen attention and present awareness, using the body as an anchor. It can also help students become more attuned to their bodies and notice when stress begins to accumulate before it gets overwhelming.

Students may notice particular sensations as they move their attention from one body part to another, or they may feel nothing at all. Let them know it is okay to feel what they feel, even if they feel nothing. If possible, conduct a body scan while students are lying down; it can also be conducted while students are sitting in their chairs.

1. Invite students into the practice:

If possible, ask students to move their chairs slightly away from their desks.

In this mindfulness practice, you are going to use your awareness to take a tour of your body through a guided body scan. We do a body scan to check in with our bodies with curiosity. There's no need to judge or change anything. Just notice each part of your body as it is in the present moment. In a minute I'm going to start. As you are guided through each part of the body scan, become aware of what you notice. You may notice tingling or warmth or coolness or pressure, or no sensation at all. Just become aware of what you feel (or don't feel) and move your awareness to the next part of the body as you follow my voice. If you begin to feel like it's hard to pay attention, remember that this is expected. Just notice when you are distracted and bring your attention back to your body as you are guided through the body scan.

Close your eyes or let them get sleepy and let your body relax. Feel the weight of your body on the chair or on the floor and start by taking three gentle, deep breaths. Breathe in through your nose and breathe out through your mouth, and notice how your belly rises and falls when you do this.
(Pause while you wait for three deep breaths)
Now, let your breathing return back to its natural pace.
(Pause)
Now turn your attention to your whole body. Notice your body being supported by the floor or a chair.
(Pause)
Now let's start by paying attention to your toes. Without moving them, what do you notice? You might notice tingling or warmth or coolness, or nothing at all. Whatever you feel is okay. Just notice your toes as they are.
(Pause)
Whenever you notice you are distracted, just bring your attention back to the sound of my voice directing you to notice a part of your body.
Now notice both of your feet.
(Pause)
Notice the soles of your feet and the top of your feet and your toes and your heels.
(Pause).
Move your attention up to your ankles,
(Pause)
and your shins and calves.
(Pause)
You may notice warmth or coolness or tingling. Or you may notice nothing at all. Whatever you feel is okay.
(Pause)
Now move your attention to your knees.
(Pause)

Be aware of what you notice. Notice the front of your knees and the backs of your knees and the sides of your knees. You may notice warmth or coolness or tingling, or you might notice nothing at all. Remember, it's okay not to notice anything.

Now move your attention to the tops of your legs or thighs.

(Pause)

Notice the front of your thighs and the backs of your thighs and the sides of your thighs.

(Pause)

Move your attention to your hips (pause) and your belly. Can you notice your breath as your belly rises and falls?

(Pause)

Now move your attention to your lower back,

(Pause)

and your upper back.

(Pause)

You might feel your back against the floor or your chair. You might notice warmth or tingling. Just notice your whole back.

Now turn your attention to your chest.

(Pause)

You might notice your chest rising and falling as you breathe. Let your attention ride the waves of your own breathing as you notice your chest.

Now turn your attention to your neck,

(Pause)

and your shoulders.

(Pause)

Now move your attention to your arms. Can you feel the front and the back and the sides of your arms? Do you feel them resting at your sides? Just bring your whole attention to your arms.

Now move your attention to your fingers.

(Pause).

Notice your thumbs and your second fingers, your third fingers, your fourth fingers, and your pinky fingers.

(Pause)

Notice the top of your hands and the palms of your hands.

(Pause)

Notice your wrists and your forearms and your upper arms. Can you feel the front and back and sides of your arms and hands? Do you feel them resting against your body or against the floor or your chair?

If your mind begins to wander, that's okay. Just notice that you've been distracted and bring your attention back to your body.

Now notice your whole body as you sit/lie here. Feel your whole body. Your whole body.

Now turn your attention away from your body and back to your breathing. Notice your breath coming into your body and your breath moving out of your body.

(Pause)

Now wiggle your toes and your fingers and, when you're ready, open your eyes.

2. You can invite students to complete the Body Scan Mindfulness Practice activity sheet on page 134 or 135. Depending on the grade level, the activity sheet asks students to describe how their body felt as they tried the body scan and to describe their level of attention and distraction. Students are asked to use words or images.

Voice from the Classroom: Body Scan
by Vanessa Mauro

As a teacher candidate, I introduced mindfulness and the body scan during my second practicum. My students were only seven years old and in Grade 2; I had doubts about whether they would grasp it. However, remembering how mindfulness makes me feel and how much it can help, I worked up the courage to introduce it to my class. After the first time, I took a class vote to find out if they would like to do more mindfulness. To my surprise, they all voted in favor of continuing. I started to facilitate mindfulness practices during transition times, such as after recess. I began by using simple breathing exercises that were teacher-directed. I would urge the class to pay attention to their breathing and the way it made them feel. I encouraged them to relax and pay attention to their lungs, envisioning them expanding and contracting. I would say, "Close your eyes and picture your lungs growing larger as you take a deep breath in. Now, breathe out and picture your lungs getting smaller. Remember how lucky you are to have lungs to help you breathe each and every day." Later, I would tell them to close their eyes and focus on all of the parts of their body, from their toes to the top of their heads. For the body scan I would simply say, "Picture your energy as a green, glowing light inside of you. Pay attention to your toes right now and picture the green light in your toes. Now, feel all of your energy move from your toes to your ankles, up to your legs, in your torso, to your chest, shoulders, arms, hands, fingers, and back up to your neck and head." I would say this statement very slowly, giving them time to feel their own energy in each body part.

I would play relaxing music in the background as students practiced. I also performed a guided practice to help students envision an oasis of natural beauty. I did this by speaking out loud to them and describing a vision of nature I believed would help boost their mood and relax them. Eventually, I took a step back and students learned how to practice mindfulness all on their own. After a very short time of teacher-directed practice, they were able to take mindfulness seriously and practice by themselves. I would simply monitor the time and ring a bell at the end. I invited them to reflect on the way that mindfulness made them feel and to write down some of their thoughts. After reading some of their responses, I was happy and surprised to see how deeply they reflected on their experience. They wrote about being able to listen to their bodies and about feeling balanced. One particular response stood out to me, as a student wrote about listening to her heart. This and other reactions moved me and I felt honored to be the one to introduce my students to something that would have a lasting impact. I am very excited to introduce mindfulness practice to my future students.

Be the Mountain

One of my first mindfulness experiences was through the Mountain Meditation by Jon Kabat-Zinn (1995). Modified versions of this are now a staple and are favorites for me and my students. As a mindfulness practice, it helps students transport their understanding of the inner stability and grounding qualities of the mountain into their own experience. Mountains that have stood tall and majestic for thousands of years have endured countless seasons of rain, snow, hail, and tumultuous storms. Still, the mountain shows unwavering resolve and stays grounded and steady in the wake of the elements that come and go. Through it all, it remains its essential self. This mindfulness practice teaches students that their thoughts and the inevitable changes and challenges of their lives are temporary. Over time, they learn to find stability in understanding their essential self is unchanged, regardless of the challenges and chaos they may be confronted with.

1. Invite students to sit in their chairs or on the floor. If this is not possible, students can lie on the floor.
2. For students who may never have seen a mountain, it is helpful to introduce an image or visual of a mountain before beginning this practice.
3. Invite students into the practice:

> *Today we are going to do a mindfulness practice called Be the Mountain. Start by closing your eyes or letting them get sleepy. Place a hand on your belly and take a few mindful breaths. Breathe in through your nose and out through your mouth.*
> (Pause)
> *Notice how this feels in your body and how your hand rises when you breathe in and falls when you breathe out. Just notice your belly and ride the waves of your breathing.*
> (Pause)
> *Now turn your attention to your body as you sit in your chair. Imagine there is a string of the top of your head and it's pulling you up just a little straighter. Notice your feet as they touch the floor and think about the way the ground supports you in your chair.*
> *Now, as you sit here, think of a beautiful, majestic mountain. It could be one you have seen before or one that you can imagine now.*
> (Pause)
> *Notice the details of your mountain.*
> (Pause)
> *How many peaks do you see at the top of your mountain?*
> (Pause)
> *Do you notice trees on your mountain? Do you see grass or flowers? Can you see snow at the top of your mountain?*
> (Pause)
> *Are there paths for people to walk or waterfalls?*
> (Pause)
> *Now, imagine your mountain has been sitting here for thousands of years. Think of all of the weather it has experienced over these years. Sun and warmth, rain and hail, wind and snow, and terrible storms. And still, it sits here steady and strong. Now bring your awareness back to yourself sitting in your chair or on the floor.*
> (Pause)
> *Imagine that you become the mountain. Through all of the changes and challenges in your life, you stay strong and steady and grounded. Just like the mountain is still the mountain, you are still you.*
> (Pause)
> *Now, turn your attention to your breathing. Notice your breath coming into your body and moving out of your body. Notice your belly rising and falling keep your awareness here until you hear the sound of the bell.*

4. You can invite students to complete the Be the Mountain activity sheet on page 136 and to record, in either words or images, how they experienced and/or what they learned from the Be the Mountain activity.

Favorite Place

This type of guided meditation is a favorite among students because it invites them to use visualization and their imaginations to think about or create a favorite/special place. Students will often return to this favorite place when they have a need for predictability, safety and security, and a feeling of control. It also gives students an opportunity to be creative.

You will find scripts for both an introductory and longer version of the Favorite Place guided practice. Use whichever script makes most sense for your classroom context.

1. If possible, invite students to lie comfortably on the floor. Students may also sit in their chairs.
2. Invite students into the Introductory Favorite Place practice:

Let your body get comfortable in your chair and let your shoulders drop. Relax your jaw and let your mouth open just slightly. Imagine there is a string at the top of your head and it's pulling your back up a little straighter. Both feet are touching the ground and your hands are on your lap. Gently let your eyes close and start by taking three nice, deep breaths. Be sure to breathe in through your nose and out through your mouth.

(Pause)

Now keep your awareness on your breathing and continue breathing naturally by allowing your breath to find its own rhythm.

Today you are invited to use your imaginations to make pictures in your mind and to go to a favorite place. Let's start by creating some pictures in your mind of a place where you feel comfortable and happy. This could be a favorite place you've been to before. Or it could be a place that you've seen. It can also be a place that's completely made up by you. Just picture a place where you feel relaxed and calm.

Now let's go ahead and add some details to your favorite place. What do you notice there? What do you see?

(Pause)

What do you smell?

(Pause)

What can you hear?

(Pause)

What is the temperature like there?

(Pause)

How do you feel in this place? How does your body feel? Are you feeling relaxed and calm?

Go ahead and stay in your place for a while. Keep noticing your environment and how it feels. Just enjoy your time here for a few moments before we have to go.

(Pause for 30 seconds or more)

Now, bring your awareness back to your breathing again. Just notice your breath as it comes into your body and moves out of your body.

(Pause for a few breaths)

With your eyes still closed, begin by noticing your body as you sit here. Feel the weight of it in your chair and your feet against the floor. Continue to notice your breathing and in a moment I will ring the bell. When you can no longer hear the sound of the bell, open your eyes.

Or choose the Extended Favorite Place lesson:

Let your body get comfortable in your chair and let your shoulders drop. Relax your jaw and let your mouth open just slightly. Imagine there is a string at the top of your head and it's pulling your back up a little straighter. Both feet are touching the ground and your hands are on your lap. Gently let your eyes close and start by taking three nice, deep breaths. Be sure to breathe in through your nose and out through your mouth.

(Pause)

Now keep your awareness on your breathing. Continue breathing naturally by allowing your breath to find its own rhythm.

Today you are invited to use your imaginations to make pictures in your mind and to go to a special place. It could be a place that you have been to before or one that you create in your mind. We'll get there in a minute. For now, let's start by imagining you are sitting in a field. Imagine you are surrounded by tall grass, sweet-smelling flowers, majestic trees that create just enough shade for you to feel comfortable under, under a bright shining sun. You feel a gentle breeze against your face and hear the sound of birds singing. You feel peaceful and happy.

As you look to the hills in the distance, you notice there's a winding pathway leading to a gate. You gently stand and begin walking on the pathway toward the gate. As you walk, the cooling breeze is waving the grass along the way and gently rustling the trees.

As you reach the gateway, you notice there is a bright golden key lying on the path below. You reach down to pick it up and notice your initials have been carved into it. This is your key and it will open your gate to lead you to your special/favorite place.

You take one deep, quiet breath in and out, and then use the key to unlock the gate. You slowly push the gate open and enter into your space.

This space is yours. There may be a pond or a river or an ocean. There may be trees or hills or mountains. There may be animals and birds. There may be a beautiful garden. There may be a hammock swinging in the breeze between two trees. Your space can look and feel however you would like. Take a few moments to explore your space.

(Pause)

You now realize it's almost time to go. This is okay, though, because you can return any time you'd like. Take one more look around you as you breathe in and out. Standing up, you begin to walk out through the gate. You retrace your steps back to where you started and sit back down.

(Pause)

Now bring your awareness back to your breathing again. Just notice your breath as it comes into your body and moves out of your body.

(Pause for a few breaths)

With your eyes still closed, begin by noticing your body as you sit here. Feel the weight of it in your chair and your feet against the floor. Continue to notice your breathing, and in a moment I will ring the bell. When you can no longer hear the sound of the bell, open your eyes.

This step is optional for either the Introductory or Extended Favorite Place lesson.

3. You can invite students to complete the Favorite Place activity sheet on page page 137 or 138. Depending on the grade level, the activity sheet asks students to describe what their favorite place looked like and how it made them feel. Students are asked to use words or images.

Voice from the Classroom: Guided Relaxation
by Marianna Trajceski

During my 14-year career as an elementary school teacher, I have always found the transitional time after lunch especially challenging. Students enter the classroom filled with joy, or filled with conflict that makes them riled up with frustration and anger. When conflict happens, they understandably want to discuss the events. But even a short discussion with students who are upset can be nearly impossible when emotions are high. As an educator, my instinct is to intervene, but I'm also aware that there are lessons to teach. In times of conflict, I'm also aware of my own frustration and my increased state of anxiety. So in order to support their emotional state and mine before moving on to our afternoon, I guide them through a simple guided mindfulness practice.

I ask students to find a comfortable spot sitting on their chair or the carpet, or lying down (most choose lying down) and to take a few deep breaths. I remind them about the difference between chest breathing and deep diaphragm breathing, and then I play some relaxing music from YouTube. Once we are comfortable, the visualization and progressive relaxation begin.

I often wing it and change the script slightly each time, but it goes something like this:

> *Start at your toes. Wiggle them a little. Tighten up your feet and then relax. Pay attention to what it feels like when they are tight and then when they are relaxed. Now imagine a light energy travelling up to your ankles. Give your ankles a little wiggle and relax. The energy continues to flow up your legs to your knees. If you find your mind wandering with thoughts or worries imagine putting them in a bubble and blowing them away…*

I continue like this for all the main body parts. Once in a while I remind them about their breathing (in through the nose for 4 seconds, then out through the mouth for 5) and about their wandering thoughts or pressing worries. They seem to really like the visualization of putting a worry in a bubble and blowing it away.

Initially many kids are silly and giggle while sitting next to each other and closing their eyes. This is new for them. Some take it very seriously and even fall asleep by the end. Gently remind students they need to be mindful of others to be sure they don't interrupt their concentration. As mindfulness practice becomes routine, more students become accustomed to it and are less disruptive.

If you are uncomfortable making up your own script, there are a number of progressive relaxation videos you can play for your students. I feel it's more effective and meaningful, though, when they hear their own teacher doing the talking. It also allows you to control the pace and length, depending on the energy level of your students on that day.

This mindfulness practice has been a lifesaver for me and for my students on more than a few occasions. After just a few moments of this practice, we can often think more clearly, rather than reacting immediately to frustration or a stressful situation. Sometimes this is all that's needed and we move on with the lesson. Other times we follow up with a discussion of the issues, especially if they seem to affect most of the group. Once they are in a calm state, it is much easier for students to problem-solve together.

Don't be afraid to give this a try. We often think there isn't time in our busy days, but if your students are not in a good frame of mind, it's likely the lesson isn't going to be successful anyway. It's definitely worth the few minutes!

Voice from the Classroom: Guided Mindfulness Stories
by Kara Dymond

"Is it longer today? Last time it was too short!"

Students nestle into their beanbags, savoring the chance to lie down and sprawl out. One boy grabs his jacket and gingerly places it over his face, as he does every time. Around the room, all eyes are closed and hands are on bellies, measuring breathing. Within seconds, we are collectively imagining what it's like to fly on a magic carpet, or to visit some secret, special place of our own design.

I first introduced mindfulness into my classroom about five years ago. I teach social thinking and self-regulatory skills in an alternative program for junior and intermediate students with high-functioning autism. Some students also have co-morbid conditions, presenting with anxiety, aggression, hyperactivity, and/or inattention. I was curious to see whether mindfulness would have any impact on my students' abilities to self-regulate. There were certainly days we'd all welcome a moment of peace!

Our daily schedule has a built-in gentle start to help students transition into the classroom and the different expectations in my room. So my mindfulness program is strategically placed as an entry point into our afternoon from the inevitable squabbles and chaos of lunch recess. I start with small steps, beginning with shorter exercises, like listening to the tone of a bell until we can no longer hear any sound. I experiment with breathing exercises, body scans, and short meditations; like most teachers, I find scripts online, write my own, or find YouTube videos. It's never long before students remind me, pre-emptively, to not forget mindfulness or even request a longer meditation. Gradually we stretch the amount of time we focus, working our way up to well over ten minutes. Sometimes I ask students to draw or write about where they most liked to go in their minds. My oldest students have written and recorded their own guided meditations, to which I have added soothing music and a gong sound effect. We then enjoy them as a class. Like clockwork, each day, students eagerly adjust to a comfortable position and close their eyes when it is time for mindfulness.

Through these exercises I have discovered how much more expressive my students can become. After each session, we share as a group how each person is feeling. Students surprise me by drawing on nuanced language and descriptions that are dramatically different from the adjectives used during our daily sharing at the Feelings Board, where they tend to rely on basic emotions, such as happy, sad, or mad and require prompting to elaborate. After a guided meditation in which we imagined releasing worries as we breathed out bubbles, students shared the creative details they had added, such as watching a rainbow of bubbles floating away. One student imagined ice-cream–flavored bubbles. I jotted notes as students expressed how they "imagined all the bubbles were all my tensions and worries"; another felt "happy [that] worries have flown away"; while a third student made the profound observation that "bubbles are like worries—meant to happen, but not to last."

When I first began mindfulness practices, I knew something was certainly working, but I wasn't quite sure what. I had students fill out Tickets-out-the-Door at the end of the day so that I could ascertain what it was that they liked about our mindfulness program. Across the board, students reported a peaceful state of being. One student wrote that, after a guided meditation, he "could breath normally."

Of all the techniques we have tried, my students have gravitated most to guided meditations. They seem to appeal most to students when they incorporate a sense of adventure and discovery. I deliberately select meditations that allow for some freedom of imagination. I take long pauses to let students explore in their minds. We follow up by discussing individual experiences, supporting a curriculum focus on different perspectives and unique ways of thinking.

During these discussions, I was shocked to find that the two students who struggled the most with inattention during lessons and work periods were, instead, hyper-focused during guided meditations. They recounted the most vivid details found in all the accounts, relishing in the retelling and the strength of their imaginations. In contrast, during read-alouds, neither of these students could sustain attention or recall details about the story past the first page, no matter how animated I was or how terrific the story. A niggling started somewhere in my brain. How could I harness this? During our next read-aloud, I told students to imagine the words I was reading like a movie in their mind, just as they would during mindfulness. The Child and Youth Worker I work with gaped at me as students began answering questions on the spot, able to discuss character and plot elements in detail. They were no longer saying they could not remember, did not know, or had not been listening. This year, with my oldest group of students, I began to read a much longer novel (*Wonder* by R.J. Palacio). Students were riveted and complained when I stopped reading. Gone are the glazed looks and voices blurting out, "I'm bored!" It is a very different picture from what it once was.

Guided meditations are now a regular part of my practice. I remember starting out thinking that mindfulness might help my students. It has had a profound impact on everyone in my classroom, including me. We're calmer. Throughout the day, we focus more intently, enjoy learning more, and are more flexible with the schedule. We may stop for a mindful moment at other times, if we feel like it. We can do more, it seems, this way. The daily opportunity to share our imaginations has helped students to express feelings more clearly and more often and, most importantly, we've all learned to listen to and appreciate one another.

Body Scan: K–Grade 2

Name: _____   Date: _____

You just tried a body scan mindfulness practice. Circle or color how this practice made you feel?

Imagine the picture below is your body. Use the space below to describe how your body felt as you tried the body scan. You may use words and/or colors.

Pembroke Publishers ©2019 *Fostering Mindfulness* by Shelley Murphy ISBN 978-1-55138-340-8

Body Scan: Grades 3–6

Name: _____   Date: _____

When you do a body scan, you pay careful attention to what you notice about your each part of your body as you take a tour from top to bottom.

1. What was it like to try the body scan?

2. What part of your body did you notice the most? The least?

On the outline below, mark the parts of your body that you were most able to keep your attention on without being distracted. If you noticed any sensations or feelings in parts of your body, write words to describe them below.

Pembroke Publishers ©2019 *Fostering Mindfulness* by Shelley Murphy ISBN 978-1-55138-340-8

Be the Mountain

Name: _____   Date: _____

You just tried a Be the Mountain mindfulness practice. Did it make you think about how weather comes and goes and the mountain remains steady and strong? What did you learn about yourself from the mountain meditation? Use the space below to describe the mountain you imagined and what you learned.

Pembroke Publishers ©2019 *Fostering Mindfulness* by Shelley Murphy ISBN 978-1-55138-340-8

Favorite Place: K–Grade 2

Name: _____   Date: _____

How did this Favorite Place mindfulness practice make you feel?

Use words and/or pictures to describe what your favorite place looked like in your mind.

Favorite Place: Grades 3–6

Name: _____   Date: _____

Take a few moments to think about the space you created for yourself within the mindfulness practice. What words or images come to mind? In the space below, describe and/or draw any of the details you remember and how being in this space made you feel.

8

Mindfulness and the Peace Corner

What Is a Peace Corner?

A Peace Corner is a dedicated space within the classroom that is also sometimes called the Calm Corner. The concept was originally pioneered by peace educator Linda Lantieri. It is a structured space that gives students the opportunity to self-regulate in times of mounting distress; it is a way for students to redirect themselves back to the rhythm of the school day. Typically, this space has a few comfortable options for sitting (cushions, beanbags), along with sensory calming tools and activities.

For many of our students, the rigor and stimulation of the school day can put their nervous systems on overdrive. When this happens, thinking and learning often take a backseat. Students may begin to feel grumpy, distracted, or increasingly agitated. When students learn to notice when they are becoming overstimulated or dysregulated, they can elect to go into this space to help calm themselves before a potential escalation or outburst. The Peace Corner, then, quickly becomes associated with calmness, independence, and agency. Students also associate the space with safety and self-care. The ultimate goal is for students to begin a habit of recognizing when they are beginning to feel dysregulated or upset and to recognize what they can do to support their well-being. Students often report that they transfer and integrate this self-awareness and self-care strategy use into their lives outside of the classroom.

The Peace Corner space does not need to be large. It simply needs to be a dedicated space where students are able to find a peaceful space with tools and resources to help them self-regulate. I like to introduce Peace Corner tools and strategies in the same way I introduced centre activities. I would never set up stations or centres and expect students to be able to work with the activities thoughtfully and independently without first ensuring they practiced and understood what was expected of them. Typically, I would introduce activities for each centre over time and allow students to become familiar with them before unveiling them for independent work. I like to introduce the tools and strategies within the Peace Corner in this same way. For example, students like to use something called a Mind Jar (see below). I begin by introducing the concept of the Mind Jar as a whole-class activity. Once students are familiar and comfortable with this activity, it can graduate to become part of the Peace Corner. This helps assure students are able to use the Mind Jar independently.

Tips for Creating and Using a Peace Corner

- Peace Corners are most effective when the space is co-constructed and designed with students. It is imperative that this space never be used in a punitive way (i.e., as a timeout). The intention is for students to make a strong association between this space and peace, calm, autonomy, and self-regulation.
- Once students become familiar with the Peace Corner and its purpose, the goal is for them to notice when they are beginning to feel dysregulated and to self-refer to this space.
- Initially, students may be guided or invited into the Peace Corner: "Cynthia, you seem like you're getting a little upset. Do you think it might be helpful to spend some time in the Peace Corner?"
- As teachers know, novelty breeds great interest. Once the newness of the Peace Corner wears off, I find that the students who use it most are the ones who need it most.
- It is helpful to remind students that the Peace Corner should not be considered an option for getting out of learning activities.
- At times it might be appropriate to allow two students to use the Peace Corner, but only if they are clear on the expectations. I decide on a case-by-case basis.
- Examples of some things you may want to include in your Peace Corner: timer, pillows, beanbags, blankets, fidget tools, mindfulness activities, emotion anchor charts, coloring materials, student-made books, favorite objects or photos, a Mind Jar, a Hoberman breathing sphere, themed books (on feelings, self-regulation, mindfulness, etc.), a Worry Box, family photos, pinwheels, student work, etc.

After the initial novelty of the Peace Corner wears off, students typically spend 5 to 10 minutes in this space. It is helpful, however, to include a simple timer for some students. You may want to prompt certain students to set the timer if they need a firm reminder and boundary of time. If more time is needed, they can negotiate this with you.

Mind Jar

Use scripts as a guide. You may read as-is or modify to fit your needs.

A Mind Jar has many names. It has been called a Glitter Jar, Calming Jar, Glitter Bottle, and Mind in a Jar, to name a few. Regardless of its name, it is an excellent visual metaphor for teaching the passing states of the mind. It is also used by students to help bring awareness to their breath as they watch the falling sparkles and calm their minds. This activity is a student favorite and is especially supportive for students who are visual and tactile learners.

Once the jar is shaken, the stirred-up glitter represents our busy and chaotic minds. As the jar becomes still, the settling sparkles represent our settling minds. When all of the sparkles have reached the bottom and the water is clear, this represents a state of calm.

The Mind Jar can also be used as a visual timer for mindful breathing exercises. I like to put just enough glycerin in the water so it takes about a minute and a half for the sparkles to settle. Students are then prompted to focus on their breathing until the sparkles settle, giving them just enough time to calm their nervous systems while focusing on their breath.

1. Create your Mind Jar.

   What you'll need:
   - Plastic or mason jar, plastic water bottle, spice jar, etc.
   - Glitter (smaller glitter is best)
   - 3-4 drops of dish soap
   - Glycerin (to slow down the fall of the glitter)
   - Warm water

   What you do:
   - Begin with a measure of 2/3 water and 1/3 glycerin.
   - Heat the water and whisk with glycerin in a bowl.
   - Add glitter and continue to whisk.
   - When the water, glycerin, and glitter are well mixed, pour the mixture into the jar or bottle.
   - Add two drops of liquid soap.
   - Put the lid on the jar and shake. If the sparkles settle too quickly, add more glycerin.
   - Leave the lid off until the water cools to room temperature.
   - Secure your lid and shake.

2. Before introducing the Mind Jar to students, I read *Moody Cow Meditates* or *Peaceful Piggy Meditation* by Kerry Lee MacLean to students. *Moody Cow Meditates* is a story about a cow who has a bad day and then learns from his grandfather how to settle his mind and let go of his frustration through a meditation glitter jar. It is a student favorite and is an excellent entry point for talking about how and why to use the mind jar.

3. Begin the lesson:

   When we get very distracted or we feel upset or angry, our minds can become cloudy. This makes it difficult to think clearly and make good decisions. When we practice mindfulness, it helps our minds to settle, so they become less cloudy and we can think more clearly and make better decisions.

   This is a Mind Jar. When the Mind Jar is shaken, the sparkles represent your thoughts and emotions when they are stirred up. Maybe you got into an argument with a friend before school.
   (Shake the mind jar)
   You forgot your homework in the car.
   (Shake the mind jar)
   Your teacher is sick and you have a substitute.
   (Shake the jar)
   It's difficult to see through the bottle because the sparkles, just like your thoughts and feelings, are swirling because you are upset or angry and you cannot think clearly. It's hard to make good decisions when we aren't thinking clearly, isn't it?
   (Continue to move the mind jar)
   Now let's think of one thing we can do with the mind jar to help the glitter settle to the bottom.
   (Pause for responses)
   Yes, we can stop moving it or hold it still. When we allow the jar to be still, the sparkles slowly settle to the bottom and we can soon see through it clearly. This is the

same for us. When we are still and we focus on our breathing, it helps our thoughts and feelings settle. They don't disappear, but they are no longer in the way and stopping us from seeing clearly. This helps us to feel calm. When you are still and calm, you can think better and make wiser choices.

Now let's do some mindful breathing together while we use the mind jar.

4. Shake the jar and invite students to begin to focus on their breathing as they watch the sparkles fall. They should continue to focus on their breath until all the sparkles have fallen to the bottom.
5. You can invite students to complete the Mind Jar activity sheet on page 150, to illustrate how their mind felt before mindfulness and how it feels after mindfulness using words and images.
6. Consider placing the Instructions for Using the Mind Jar activity sheet on page 151 in the Peace Corner for students' reference.

Mindful Coloring

Coloring books are everywhere and not just for children anymore. Look around any bookstore and you will find a dedicated section specifically for adults. Perhaps this is because there are research findings to back the therapeutic benefits of coloring for adults. In a study of nearly 200 Grade 8 students who colored just before a test, there was a significant decrease in test anxiety and a significant increase in states of mindfulness (Carsley, & Heath, 2018). Students not only reap the rewards of the mindfulness aspect of coloring, but coloring also helps to improve motor skills, stimulate creativity, improve focus and hand–eye coordination, and strengthen their awareness of structure and spatial awareness. All of this makes a compelling case for coloring!

Mindful coloring gives students an opportunity to focus their attention on the present through a simple repetitive task. Mindfulness is not built into the coloring activity itself. The mindfulness practice comes through the quality of attention students bring to their coloring. In mindful coloring, students are asked to choose and apply a color in a design. While a byproduct of mindful coloring is that it helps to take students' minds off something that may be dysregulating them (fear, anger, anxiety), its purpose is to give students an opportunity to focus their attention. In this way, the coloring becomes the anchor within the mindfulness practice.

1. Copy a Mindful Coloring template from page 152 or 153. These activity sheets can be used as templates for coloring. The image on page 152 can be used by older students, while the image on page 153 can be used by K–Grade 2 students.
2. Have pencil crayons and fine markers available for student use.
3. Begin by introducing the practice of mindful coloring. It is helpful to distinguish between mindful coloring and simple coloring. If students are lost in thought or daydreaming while they color, it is not a mindfulness practice. If they are focused on the details of the experience, such as the way the pencil crayons or the paper feel in their hands, the movement of their fingers as they apply color to the design, or the rhythm of their breath as they focus their attention on the task at hand, then coloring is a mindfulness practice. As with other mindfulness practices, when students notice they are

no longer focusing on their coloring, this means their mind has wandered and they should bring their awareness back to the task at hand.

4. Model what it looks like to color mindfully. This can be done as simply as drawing some small shapes on the board to color mindfully.

5. Mindful coloring can be done as a whole-class activity or offered as an option when some students need to self-regulate; e.g., for use in the Peace Corner.

6. One Mindful Coloring template can be used over an extended period, as it can take quite a bit of time to complete.

Mindfulness Cootie Catcher

A cootie catcher, also known as a paper fortuneteller, is a form of origami used by students to play. Most often, students play in partners, but a cootie catcher can be enjoyed individually as well. While one student holds the cootie catcher, the other chooses names or numbers to reveal a hidden message. A Mindfulness Cootie Catcher is used by students to reveal a message that suggests a particular mindfulness practice. Think of keeping one in the Peace Corner and giving students the opportunity to make one to bring home.

1. Copy the Mindfulness Cootie Catcher Template on page 154 and the Make and Play with Your Mindfulness Cootie Catcher activity sheet on page 155 for each student. Copy on separate sheets of paper, not double-sided, as one will need to be cut out.

2. Have scissors available for your students to cut their templates. You may wish to precut the templates for younger students.

3. Model each folding step for your students until their cootie catcher is complete.

4. With students, go over the steps for how to play with their cootie catcher, as outlined in the Make and Play with Your Mindfulness Cootie Catcher activity sheet on page 155. It can be helpful to model how to play with one of your students.

5. Let the playing begin.

Self-Care in the Peace Corner

Self-Care Anchor Chart

I like the idea of working with students to co-construct ideas for tools and strategies within the Peace Corner. Once they have learned about and are comfortable with a few mindfulness strategies, I generate an anchor chart with the whole class. This anchor chart then hangs somewhere within the Peace Corner to help prompt students to use some of the strategies for self-care.

1. After introducing students to several mindfulness strategies, activities, and techniques, invite them to help you create a list of those that have been most enjoyable and helpful for them.

2. Record on chart paper.

3. Place the Self-Care Anchor Chart within the classroom, perhaps in the Peace Corner.

4. Remind students that they can refer to this chart for tools or strategies for self-care at any point throughout the day, especially when they are beginning to feel dysregulated, upset, stressed, angry, etc.

Voice from the Classroom: Mindfulness and the Peace Corner
by Colleen Cowan

Mindfulness has had a profound impact on my personal mental health by providing a wonderful coping strategy for managing my stress and anxiety and for tapping into my sense of gratitude. Considering how important it has become to me, I decided to introduce the concept to my students during my practicum placements as a teacher candidate.

My first placement was in a Kindergarten class. The children were very busy and I was reluctant to attempt to bring in quiet mindful moments for fear of failing. I started by reading the book *Silence* by Lemniscates, which is about listening to the sounds around us. Following the read-aloud, I conducted a brief mindful listening exercise and had students tell me about what they heard when their eyes were closed. At first, the experience wasn't as successful as I had hoped; there was a lot of giggling and shuffling, which I expected. I attempted to try mindfulness again and, this time, from a different angle. This time I focused on feelings like sadness and anger. The students were more receptive to this and our discussion on feelings and using mindfulness to help them feel balanced again led to the creation of their Calm Corner. On clouds, students wrote calming words and things to think about to help them relax. They came up with beautiful ideas like *hug my mom, play with my sister, doing yoga*. Although initially reluctant, I was proud of the way mindfulness evolved in the classroom and how easily it was implemented. This experience also taught me to be more flexible in my approaches to mindfulness—the first attempt did not work and the second was better.

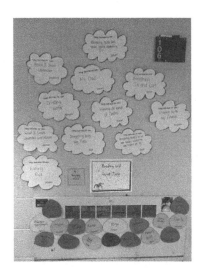

My second placement was in a Grade 1 classroom and, having confidence from the success of my previous implementation, I introduced mindfulness almost immediately. However, this classroom was different from the first, in that students needed mindfulness in order to better relate to each other. I presented mindfulness as a way for them to become better aware of their words and actions inside and outside the classroom. I read *Peaceful Piggy Meditation* by Kerry Lee MacLean as an introduction the concept of being kind to one another. We also created a kindness garden: students made handprint flowers with a partner and recorded qualities of a good friend directly on the flower pots. Some students wrote *listening to each other* and *playing with everyone*. We also created a kindness jar for students to recognize when others had done nice things. For each nice thing, a stone was placed in the jar to represent an act of kindness. The goal was to fill the jar. The students were very receptive to these activities that helped them to be mindful of their words and actions. The associate teacher made a comment about the classroom environment being much improved by the end of my four weeks.

Through my experiences, I have seen how mindfulness can affect people of all ages. I have been inspired by seeing how a brief daily practice can have such an impact. One of my most treasured moments was when a student in my Grade 1 class came back from recess crying because another student had upset her. She said, "I know she didn't mean it; she's just tired." In response, another student came over with the glitter bottle, gave it to the upset student, and said, "I hope you feel better." I will always remember this moment and the pride I felt because I knew these students were beginning to truly understand the power of mindfulness.

Recording Self-Care in the Peace Corner

It is helpful to keep track of which students are using the Peace Corner and how often. You may invite students to respond in writing to their experiences of being in the Peace Corner. This will give you a sense of the strategies students are electing to use and how they are experiencing them. This can also serve as an excellent reminder for students of the purpose of the Peace Corner.

1. Once students have learned a handful of mindfulness strategies, photocopy the Self-Care in the Peace Corner activity sheet on page 156. Have this activity sheet available in a designated spot in your classroom, preferably in the Peace Corner.
2. Provide an overview of this activity sheet for your students in preparation for their future use. Explain that, on this activity sheet, they are asked to describe what strategy or strategies they used to take care of themselves and how they felt afterward.
3. Invite students to complete the Self-Care in the Peace Corner activity sheet after a Peace Corner visit.
4. Students may submit the activity sheet to you or place in a designated private mailbox.
5. Congratulate students on their choice to use strategies to take care of themselves and to self-regulate.

Voice from the Classroom: On Having a Peace Corner in the Classroom

by Carmen Wai

I have taught a number of different grades (Kindergarten to Grade 6) in a number of different contexts (Special Education classes, ESL classes). In every context, mindfulness has transformed the dynamics of our classroom and even provided a space for healing. There are no right or wrong ways to set up a Peace Corner. In every classroom I have taught, the Peace Corner has looked very different. I simply ask myself whether or not our Peace Corner serves the needs of my particular group of students, feels peaceful, and is perceived as a safe space.

I often begin with a read-aloud and a classroom discussion about peace. There are many great books about peace, such as *The Peace Book* by Todd Parr and *I Am Peace: A Book of Mindfulness* by Susan Verde. As a class, we sometimes make our own peace book to add to the space. In our discussions, students always bring up the word "quiet" in relation to "peace." We talk about the Peace Corner being a quiet space in which we care for ourselves and others.

It is easy to overcrowd your Peace Corner with too many items, colors, and images. I find it is important to ensure that my Peace Corner actually feels peaceful. Often, less is more, depending on what students need. I try to use neutral colors and to provide soft or natural lighting. I like to position the Peace Corner close to a quiet window where students can feel the sunlight, observe nature, and engage in people-watching or bird-watching. If natural light is not possible, I like using string lights or bedside lamps to provide soft lighting. To bring in elements of the outdoors, I include plants and images of nature. I often include pillows and blankets to make the space cozy and warm. I place the classroom library in this space as a quiet, calming activity; this library also includes books authored by the students. We have a number of students who have special needs. While some students find it relaxing to listen to calming music, others respond by getting overstimulated. For this reason, I provide noise-cancelling headphones and offer opportunities to listen to nature sounds and soft music.

To make this space meaningful, we have regular mindfulness practice; I place artifacts/visuals in the Peace Corner to remind students of this practice. For example, as a daily mindfulness practice we use a calming technique called Square Breaths. I place a diagram on how to take Square Breaths in this space. We also practice a calming technique during which I say, "Smell the rose (students breathe in), blow out the candle (students breathe out), and feel good (students give themselves a hug)." I include a flower, a candle, and an image of a child giving themself a hug to serve as a reminder of this practice. Other artifacts I might include are calming/glitter jars, images of nature, and tissue boxes. I also ask my students what else they might like in their Peace Corner. For a smaller class, students can all bring their own artifacts to help them feel calm and happy. For a larger class, we can co-create a photo book of artifacts.

For many of my students, the Peace Corner is a healing space. I've seen an emotionally charged twelve-year-old soothe himself into a peaceful state. Before I introduced mindfulness practice to this student and his classmates, his response to strong emotions was to harm himself or others. Having the opportunity to take some time for himself within the Peace Corner gave him a chance to return to a calmer state. It is great to see him regulate his own emotions; the environment of the Peace Corner acts as a reminder of the strategies that are available to him. I like to think that he and other students will be able to carry this safe space within their hearts and minds when they leave the classroom. A parent of a Kindergarten student once told me that her son asked her to smell the rose, blow out the candle, and feel good with him before he went to bed. It is now a part of their bedtime ritual.

Providing a space where students can practice mindfulness and self-regulation truly changes the dynamics of a classroom. One day, I noticed a crowd of students assembling in the centre of our classroom. This crowd grew bigger until almost the entire class had gathered together. As I approached to find out what the matter was, I realized my entire class of Kindergarten students had surrounded a crying classmate. They were delivering tissues and were together quietly smelling the rose (breathing in), blowing out the candle (breathing out), and giving themselves a hug. They were doing this to prompt the crying student to do the same. And she did. Mindfulness and our Peace Corner have created a safe and caring environment for all of our students. As one student said, "It makes me feel love."

Voice from the Classroom: On Having a Peace Corner in the Classroom

by Sherry-Lynne Kirschner

As teachers we are keenly aware of the importance of creating a safe environment in our classrooms to nurture the growth of our students. When we integrate mindfulness into our daily curriculum, we help our students develop valuable strategies for regulating their emotions. Students can learn that emotions are natural, transient, and part of being human. With daily practice, emotions can be observed as "easy" or "difficult" instead of judged as "good" or "bad." Through cultivating acceptance, students can learn to do the work that is necessary to transform challenging emotions like fear and anger into happiness and peace.

Creating a dedicated space for the children to practice these strategies can facilitate a deepening of their overall emotional awareness. I have found establishing a Peace Corner in my classroom to be extremely beneficial on many levels. As part of our daily mindfulness practice in the classroom, moments are spent in silent reflection. At times, students notice hovering emotions that are challenging to "sit with." As Jack Kornfield expressed so eloquently, "When we take time for quiet, what shows itself is the unfinished business of the heart. If you allow the tears, they wash you and you become kinder and more compassionate." When students have access to a private space to work with emotions that are unsettling, they develop their ability to culture their own inner resiliency. It's a place where they can cool off and practice shifting their emotions independently. In the private atmosphere of this quiet space and through the use of sensory tools, breath practice, and mindful movement, students develop and refine self-regulation skills that contribute to their overall well being.

It is essential that the guidelines for using the Peace Corner are clear and monitored closely. I have found over the years, when supporting other teachers to incorporate Peace Corners into their classrooms, that the initial stages of reinforcing clear expectations is vital to the success of the space. These expectations vary according to the developmental stage of the students, the nature of the class, and the teaching style of the educator. I have noticed that it has been helpful to integrate daily reflection on the use of the Peace Corner into my own mindfulness practice so I can make conscious, caring adjustments that are beneficial to my students' and my own personal growth. For example, one time at the end of a busy and challenging day in my classroom, some of my students informed me that they had found some stress balls had been destroyed. My initial reaction matched their feelings of irritation and resentment for the presumed lack of respect of property. Then, luckily, I was able to take a breath and remind myself that this was a call to awareness and an opportunity for clarity and compassion. I was grateful for this split second of insight, because at times it is not present and reactivity takes a front seat! I was able to investigate and discover the truth behind the event—not that I excused the infraction. However, I was able to work with the student's behavior and help her take responsibility for her actions in a calmer manner. The Peace Corner not only provides gifts for the students, but the teachers as well!

Overall expectations for all grade levels:

1. Show the peace sign when you feel you need to visit the peace corner. (I keep a close eye on the use of this at the beginning so it is not misused.)

2. Set the timer. (I usually set my own timer for one minute longer to help me keep track and allow the student the opportunity to complete the session and clean up independently.)
3. Choose the tool that is the most helpful. Be gentle and respectful.
4. Breathe and take care of your heart.
5. Replace the tool(s) you have used.
6. Congratulate yourself for your practice.
7. Return quietly to class. We are proud of your self-care!

Peace corners typically include comfortable places to sit, like beanbag chairs or a carpet with pillows. Privacy is created in an imaginative way through the use of bookshelves or hanging dividers. Storybooks and informational text that support character development and mindfulness practices can be helpful to all ages. Students of all levels also enjoy using special writing paper and pens/markers that are kept specifically for the Peace Corner. Focusing tools may vary according to the age or developmental level of the students. We know the brain loves novelty. I often rotate objects to offer a variety of ways to shift the brain to a more receptive state and help students experiment to find the most effective tool for them.

I have included a list of items that could be used at different stages of development. Obviously there is overlap and objects can be substituted and rotated according to the emotional need of student.

Early Years

- Mirror
- Concentration game (match faces showing different emotions)
- Weighted lap pillows
- Windmills or objects that promote breath practice (feathers and straws)
- Brain break cards (pictures of people jumping, yoga poses)
- Peace bottles to shake and breathe until the colors or objects settle
- Sensory mini mats (or shoeboxes) for feet or hands to feel different textures
- Tablet with calming music
- Magnetic beads
- Cotton Calming Box: a tissue box filled with cotton balls; students empty the box, count, and replace them
- Putty

Primary

- I Spy bottle: objects are placed in a plastic bottle and filled with rice; students shake until objects are spotted
- Spinning tops
- Discovery jars: filled with beans and flowers, water and mini-elastics, paper clips and magnets, water beads
- Rainsticks: made by filling a bottle with toothpicks and rice
- Mandalas to color
- Cooling-Off Cubes: plastic ice cubes with different breathing strategies written on them
- Feelings Faces to draw how they are feeling
- Sound eggs: plastic eggs filled with materials; students shake, listen, and find the match
- A Worry Box: with cards for students to write their worries on

Junior

- Slime
- Diagrams of the brain and play clay to shape the parts affected by mindfulness practice
- Beads and bracelet-making materials
- Wire for wire sculpture (Most popular activity!)
- Precious stones for practicing loving kindness
- Crocheting and knitting materials
- Rainbow elastics and loom
- Puzzles
- Diffuser with calming scents
- Optical illusion cards
- Joke books

Intermediate

- Finger mandalas
- Gratitude jar materials
- Music or guided mediation player with ear buds
- Slime or putty
- Letter-writing materials or journals
- Magazines
- Beach stones and markers
- Flip book of positive affirmations
- Rocks for rock stacking
- Inspirational videos on a tablet

In our school, we have also integrated a Mindfulness Room, which is a Peace Corner on a larger scale. It is dedicated to students or staff who are struggling through the day and need a quiet space to self-reflect out of the classroom. Some staff members meditate together in this space in the morning before school. We have found that this has had a profound impact on our school climate. When teachers find a student would benefit from the use of the space, the administrators are signalled. They accompany the student to the Mindfulness Room and provide supervision while the student practices self-regulation skills. This practice often helps to de-escalate emotions prior to discussions in the office. The space is also supervised during recess and lunch hours for students who need support.

Peace Corners and Mindfulness Rooms provide space to pause and recover from sensory overwhelm and busyness of the classroom. The quiet corner allows the brain to reboot and shift to a more receptive state for learning. In these challenging times, the Peace Corner is an essential part of the classroom that nurtures the mental health of students. In the words of a fourth grader, "The Peace Corner helps make my heart kinder."

Mind Jar

Name: _____   Date: _____

In the mind jar below, draw how your mind feels **before** mindfulness

In the mind jar below, draw how your mind feels **after** mindfulness

Write 3–5 words to describe how you feel before mindfulness:

Write 3–5 words to describe how you are feeling after mindfulness:

Pembroke Publishers ©2019 *Fostering Mindfulness* by Shelley Murphy ISBN 978-1-55138-340-8

Instructions for Using the Mind Jar

1. Begin by letting the sparkles completely settle to the bottom. Now you are ready to begin.

2. Shake the jar so the sparkles are spinning around; this is your busy mind.

3. Put the jar down and watch the sparkles fall as you focus on your breathing.

4. Continue to watch the sparkles slowly fall; as they settle to the bottom, let your mind settle and continue to focus on your breathing at the same time.

5. This is your calm mind.

Pembroke Publishers ©2019 *Fostering Mindfulness* by Shelley Murphy ISBN 978-1-55138-340-8

Mindful Coloring: Grades 3 and Up

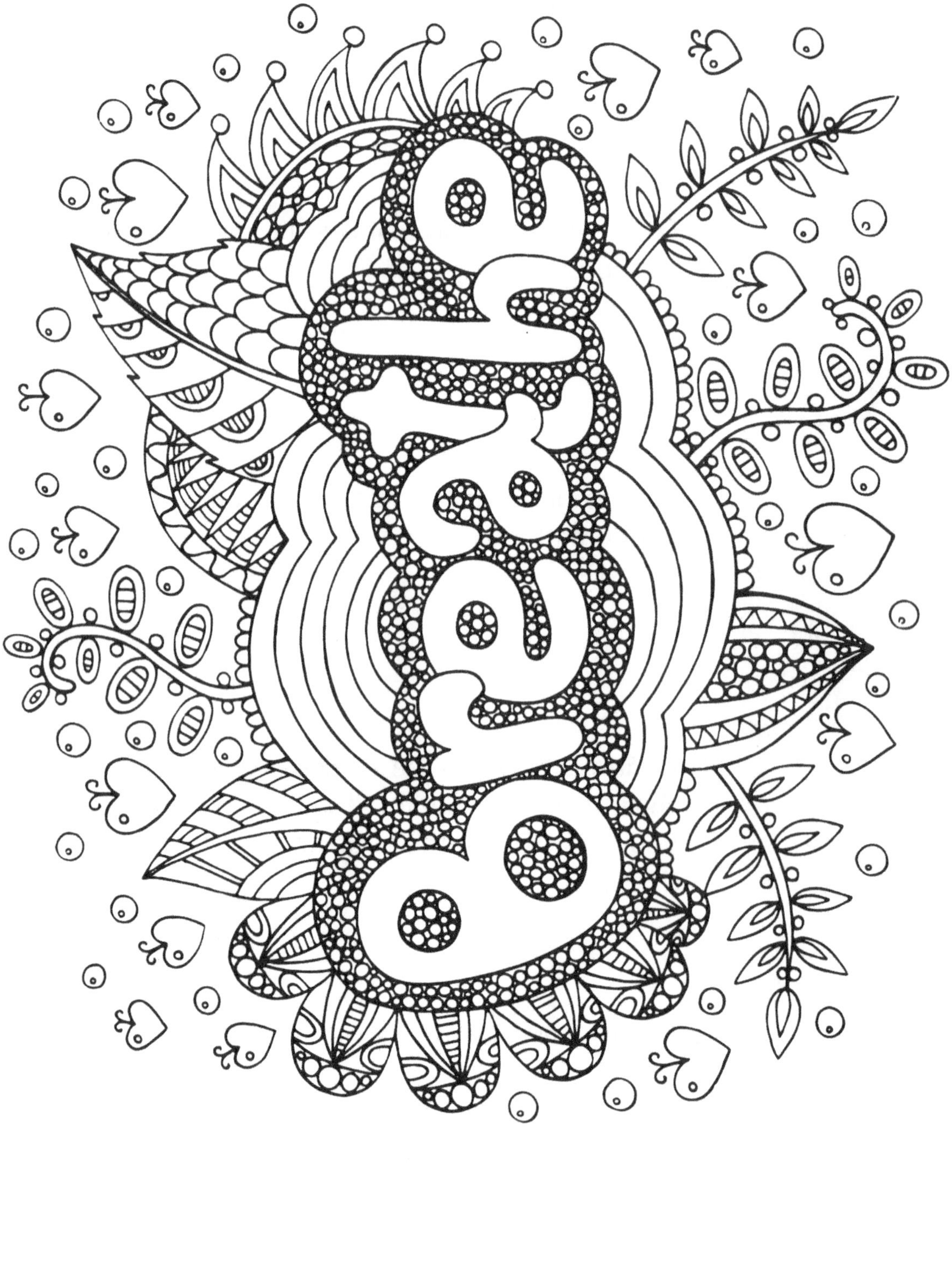

Mindfulness Cootie Catcher Template

Fold the Sheet with the lines facing down.

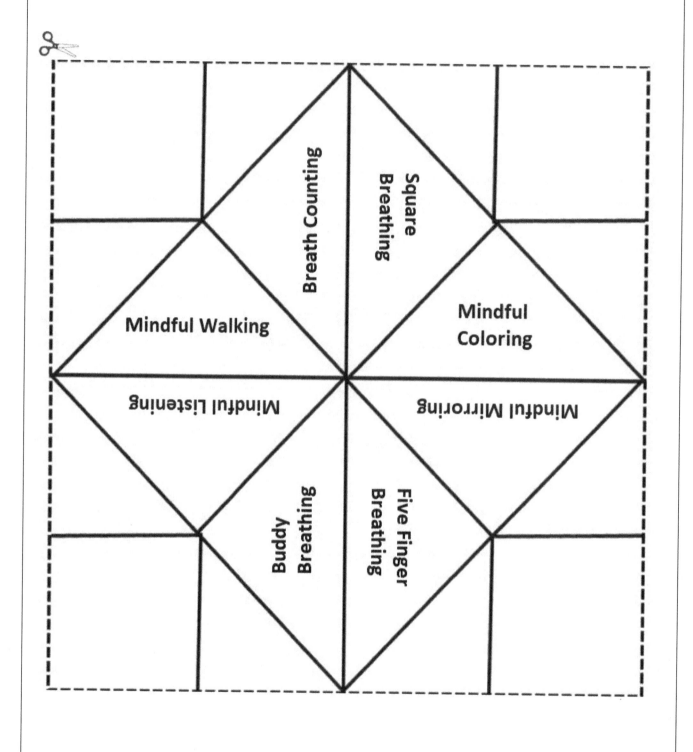

Make and Play with Your Mindfulness Cootie Catcher

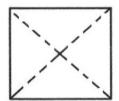

Begin with your square.

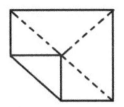

Fold each corner into the centre

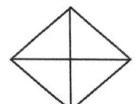

Your cootie catcher should now look like this.

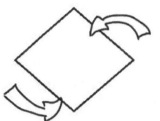

Flip the paper over so the folded sides are face down.

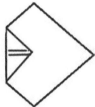

Now fold all of the corners into the center again.

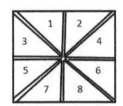

Now write numbers 1-8 on each of the triangles.

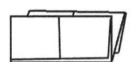

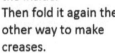

Fold the paper in half with the numbers on the inside.
Then fold it again the other way to make creases.

Slide your fingers under the 4 flaps and expand it by opening your fingers.

1. You have written numbers on the inside of your Cootie Catcher already. On each of the four outside flaps, write the name of a color (other ideas are animals, places, or people).

2. Slip your index fingers and thumbs into the flaps. While keeping the Cootie Catcher closed, ask a friend to choose one of the colors. Then spell out the color they picked, opening and closing the Cootie Catcher once for each letter in the color. Leave it open at the end so you can see the eight numbers on the inside.

3. Ask your friend to pick one of the eight numbers and open and close the Cootie Catcher that many times. Remember to leave it open at the end. Ask your friend to pick another number and open and close it that many times again.

4. Finally, ask your friend to pick a third number and lift that flap to read your message. Try this mindfulness practice with your partner or on your own.

Pembroke Publishers ©2019 *Fostering Mindfulness* by Shelley Murphy ISBN 978-1-55138-340-8

Self-Care in the Peace Corner

Name: _____   Date: _____

You just spent some time in the Peace Corner. Good for you for choosing to take care of yourself! What strategy/strategies did you use during your time in the Peace Corner?

How did it help you feel calm and ready to learn again?

Pembroke Publishers ©2019 *Fostering Mindfulness* by Shelley Murphy ISBN 978-1-55138-340-8

Resources

Recommended Resources

Read-Alouds

Mindfulness Read-Alouds

Cook, J. (2018) *Be Where Your Feet Are!* Chattanooga, TN: National Centre for Youth Issues.

DiOrio, R. (2010) *What Does It Mean To Be Present?* San Francisco, CA: Little Pickle Press.

Jordan, L. (2017) *Yawning Yoga*. San Francisco, CA: Little Pickle Press.

Kraftchuk, S. (2013) *Love to be Me!* Toronto, ON: Love to Be Publications

Kraftchuk, S. (2014) *I Am. Magical Me!* Toronto, ON: Love to Be Publications

Lemniscates (2012) *Silence*. Washington, DC: Imagination Press.

MacLean, K. L. (2004) *Peaceful Piggy Meditation*. Park Ridge, IL: Albert Whitman & Company.

MacLean, K. L. (2009) *Moody Cow Meditates*. Somerville, MA: Wisdom Publications.

Marlowe, S. (2013) *No Ordinary Apple: A Story About Eating Mindfully*. Somerville, MA: Wisdom Publications.

Verde, S. (2015) *I Am Yoga*. New York, NY: Abrams Publishing.

Verde, S. (2017) I *Am Peace: A Book of Mindfulness*. New York, NY: Abrams Publishing.

Feelings Read-Alouds

Bang, M. (2004) *When Sophie Gets Angry—Really, Really Angry*. New York, NY: Scholastic.

Coombs, K. (2017) *Breathe and Be: A Book of Mindfulness Poems*. Louisville, CO: Sounds True Inc.

Cornwall, G. (2017) *Jabari Jumps*. Somerville, MA: Candlewick Press.

de la Peña, M. (2015) *Last Stop on Market Street*. New York, NY: Penguin.

Garcia, G. (2017) *Listening to My Body: A guide to helping kids understand the connection between their sensations (what the heck are those?) and feelings so that they can get better at figuring out what they need*. Nevada City, CA: Take Heart Press.

Kraulis, J. (2013) *Whimsy's Heavy Things*. Toronto, ON: Tundra.

Ludwig, T. (2013) *The Invisible Boy*. New York, NY: Random House.

Miller, P. (2018) *Be Kind*. New York, NY: Roaring Brook Press

Moniz, M. (2017) *Today I Feel…: An Alphabet of Feelings*. New York, NY: Abrams Publishing.

Rylant, C. (2017) *Life*. San Diego, CA: Beach Lane Books.

Witek, J. (2014) *In My Heart: A Book of Feelings*. New York, NY: Abrams Publishing.

The Brain and the Senses Read-Alouds and Readers

Aliki. (2015) *My Five Senses* (Let's-Read-and-Find-Out Science 1). New York, NY: HarperCollins.

Deak, J. (2010) *Your Fantastic Elastic Brain*. San Francisco, CA: Little Pickle Press, Inc.

Isadora, R. (2016) *I Hear a Pickle: and Smell, See, Touch, Taste It, Too!* New York, NY: Nancy Paulsen Books.

Greathouse, L. (2014) *Brain* (Science Readers: A Closer Look). Huntington Beach, CA: Teacher Created Materials.

Prior, J. (2012) *The Five Senses* (TIME FOR KIDS Nonfiction Readers) 2nd Edition. Huntington Beach, CA: Teacher Created Materials.

Williams, B. (2011) *Look Inside: Your Brain* (TIME FOR KIDS Nonfiction Readers) 2nd Edition. Huntington Beach, CA: Teacher Created Materials.

Professional Resources

Mindfulness Organizations, Curriculum, and Programs

"A mindfulness-based kindness curriculum for preschoolers" Healthy Minds Innovations. https://centerhealthyminds.org/join-the-movement/sign-up-to-receive-the-kindness-curriculum (requires sign-up)

The Association for Mindfulness in Education. http://www.mindfuleducation.org/

Collaborative for Academic, Social, and Emotional Learning. https://casel.org/

The Greater Good Science Center at the University of California, Berkeley. https://greatergood.berkeley.edu/

The Hawn Foundation (2011) *The MindUP Curriculum: Grades PreK–2: Brain-Focused Strategies for Learning-and Living*. Also, *Grades 3–5* and *Grades 6–8*. New York, NY: Scholastic Teaching Resources.

Inner Kids Program. https://www.susankaisergreenland.com/inner-kids-model/

Mindful Schools. https://www.mindfulschools.org/

Mindfulness Games/Resources

Greenland, S. K. (2017). *Mindful Games Activity Cards: 55 Fun Ways to Share Mindfulness with Kids and Teens*. Boston, MA: Shambhala Publications.

Howson, S. (2002) *Manifest your Magnificence: 64 Affirmation cards for kids 6–12 years old*. Toronto, ON: Magnificent Creations Limited.

Professional Learning

Dweck, C. (2017) *Mindset—Updated Edition: Changing The Way You Think To Fulfil Your Potential.* London, UK: Little Brown.

Fitch, S. (2011) *Breathe, Stretch, Write.* Markham, ON: Pembroke.

Flippo, T. (2016) *Social and Emotional Learning in Action: Experiential Activities to Positively Impact School Climate.* Lanham, MD: Rowman & Littlefield.

Goleman, D. (2006) *Social Intelligence: The New Science of Human Relationships.* New York, NY: Bantam Dell.

Greenland, S. K. (2010) *The Mindful Child: How to Help Your Kid Manage Stress and Become Happier, Kinder, and More Compassionate.* New York, NY: Free Press.

Hanh, T. N., & Weare, K. (2017) *Happy Teachers Change the World: A Guide for Cultivating Mindfulness in Education.* Berkeley, CA: Parallax Press.

Himelstein, S. (2013) *A Mindfulness-Based Approach to Working with High-Risk Adolescents.* New York, NY: Routledge.

Jennings, P. (2015) *Mindfulness for Teachers: Simple Skills for Peace and Productivity in the Classroom* (The Norton Series on the Social Neuroscience of Education). New York: W.W. Norton & Company.

Jennings, P. (2018) *The Trauma-Sensitive Classroom: Building Resilience with Compassionate Teaching.* New York, NY: W. W. Norton & Company.

Kabat-Zinn, J. (2013) *Full Catastrophe Living: Using the Wisdom of Your Body and Mind to Face Stress, Pain, and Illness.* New York, NY: Bantam Books.

Lantieri, L. (2016) *Building Emotional Intelligence: Practices to Cultivate Inner Resilience in Children.* Louisville, CO: Sounds True Inc.

Mandel J. (2013) *Moment to Moment.* Markham, ON: Pembroke.

Mandel J. (2014) *Stop the Stress in Schools.* Markham, ON: Pembroke.

Miller, J.P. (2018) *Love and Compassion: Exploring Their Role in Education.* Toronto, ON: University of Toronto Press.

Robb, A., Strang-Campbell, E., & Calkins, L. (Ed.) (2018) *Social Issues Book Clubs: Reading for Empathy and Advocacy.* Portsmouth, NH: Heinemann.

Saltzman, A. (2014). *A Still Quiet Place: A Mindfulness Program for Teaching Children and Adolescents to Ease Stress and Difficult Emotions.* Oakland, CA: New Harbinger Publications.

Salzberg, S. (2002) *Loving-Kindness: The Revolutionary Art of Happiness.* Boston, MA: Shambhala Publications.

Siegel, D. J. (2012) *The Whole-Brain Child: 12 Revolutionary Strategies to Nurture Your Child's Developing Mind.* New York, NY: Bantam Books.

Snel, E. (2013) *Sitting Still Like a Frog: Mindfulness Exercises for Kids (and Their Parents).* Boston, MA: Shambhala Publications.

Srinivasan, M. (2014) *Teach, Breathe, Learn: Mindfulness In and Out of the Classroom.* Berkeley, CA: Parallax Press.

Willard, C. & Saltzman, A. (Eds.) (2015) *Teaching Mindfulness Skills to Kids and Teens.* New York, NY: Guilford Press.

Mindfulness Apps

The Mindfulness App. http://themindfulnessapp.com/
Headspace. https://www.headspace.com/
Calm. https://www.calm.com/
MINDBODY. https://mindbody.io/
Buddhify. https://buddhify.com/

Insight Timer. https://insighttimer.com/
Smiling Mind. https://www.smilingmind.com.au/smiling-mind-app
Meditation Timer Pro (only for Apple devices). http://www.maxwellapps.com/
apps_7_meditation_timer_pro.html
Stop, Breathe & Think. https://www.stopbreathethink.com/
10% Happier. http://www.10percenthappier.com/
Breethe. https://breethe.com/
Simply Being. https://www.meditationoasis.com/apps/

References

Black, D. S., & Fernando, R. (2014) "Mindfulness Training and Classroom Behaviour among Lower Income and Ethnic Minority Elementary School Children" *Journal of Child and Family Studies,* 23(7), 1242–1246.

Brown, K. W. & Ryan, R. M. (2003) "The Benefits of Being Present: Mindfulness and Its Role in Psychological Well-Being" *Journal of Personality and Social Psychology*, 84(4), 822–848.

Carsley, D., & Heath, N. (2018) "Effectiveness of mindfulness-based colouring for test anxiety in adolescents" *School Psychology International*, 39(3): 251–272.

Costello, E., & Lawler, M. (2014) "An exploratory study of the effects of mindfulness on perceived levels of stress among school-age children from lower socioeconomic backgrounds" *International Journal of Emotional Education*, 6(2), 21–39.

Covey, S., R. (1989) *The 7 Habits of Highly Effective People: Powerful Lessons in Personal Change.* New York, NY: Free Press.

Flook, L., Goldberg, S., Pinger, L., Bonus, K., & Davidson, R. (2013) "Mindfulness for Teachers: A pilot study to assess effects on stress, burnout and teaching efficacy" *International Mind, Brain, and Education*, 7(3): 182–195. doi: 10.1111/mbe.12026.

Garg, S. & Koenig, K. (2015) "The effectiveness of the get ready to learn program in executive functions in children with disabilities" *The American Journal of Occupational Therapy*, doi:10.5014/ajot.2015.69S1-PO2081

Goleman, D. (1995) *Emotional intelligence: Why it can matter more than IQ.* London, UK: Bloomsbury Publishing.

Greenberg M., Brown J, & Abenavoli R. (2016) "Teacher Stress and Health: Effects on Teachers, Students, and Schools" *Social Emotional Learning*, The Pennsylvania State University, 1–12.

Hanson, R., & Hanson, F. (2018) *Resilient: How to Grow an Unshakable Core of Calm, Strength, and Happiness.* New York, NY: Harmony Books.

Jha, A.P., Witkin, J.E., Morrison, A.B., Rostrup, N., & Stanley, E. (2017) "Short-Form Mindfulness Training Protects Against Working Memory Degradation over High-Demand Intervals" *Journal of Cognitive Enhancement*, 1(2): 154–171. https://doi.org/10.1007/s41465-017-0035-2.

Kabat-Zinn, J. (2013) *Full Catastrophe Living: Using the Wisdom of Your Body and Mind to Face Stress, Pain, and Illness.* New York, NY: Bantam Books.

Killingsworth, M. A., & Gilbert, D. T. (2010) "A Wandering Mind Is an Unhappy Mind" *Science*, 330(6006): 932. doi: 10.1126/science.1192439.

Klingbeil, D. A., Renshaw, T. L., Willenbrink, J. B., Copek, R. A., Chan, K. T., Haddock, A., Yassine, J., Clifton, J. (2017) "Mindfulness-based interventions with youth: A comprehensive meta-analysis of group design studies" *Journal of School Psychology*, 63, 77–103. doi: 10.1016/j.jsp.2017.03.006.

Leung, M., Chan, C. C., Yin, J., Lee, C. F., So, K.F., & Lee, T. M. (2013) "Increased grey matter volume in the right angular and posterior parahippocampal gyri in loving-kindness meditators" *Social Cognitive and Affective Neuroscience*, 8 (1): 34–39.

Leyland, A., Rowse, G., & Emerson, L. (2018) "Experimental Effects of Mindfulness Inductions on Self-Regulation: Systematic Review and Meta-Analysis" *Emotion*, 1–15. http://dx.doi.org/10.1037/emo0000425

MacDonald, H.Z. & Price, J.L. (2017) "Emotional Understanding: Examining Alexithymia as a Mediator of the Relationship Between Mindfulness and Empathy" *Mindfulness*, 8(6): 1644–1652. https://doi.org/10.1007/s12671-017-0739-5

Miller, J. P. (2018) *Love and Compassion: Exploring their Role in Education.* Toronto, ON: University of Toronto Press.

Molloy, L., Jennings, P. A., DeMauro, A. A., Mischenko P. P., & Brown, J. L. (2018) "Protective Effects of Interpersonal Mindfulness for Teachers Emotional Supportiveness in the Classroom" *Mindfulness*, 1–10. doi: 10.1007/s12671-018-0996-y.

Murphy, S. (2018) "Preparing Teachers for the Classroom: Mindful Awareness Practice in Preservice Education Curriculum" in Byrnes, K., Dalton, J. & Dorman, B. (Eds.), *Impacting Teaching and Learning: Contemplative Practices, Pedagogy, and Research in Education*, 41–51. Lanham, MD: Rowman and Littlefield.

MHASEF Research Team (2015) *The Mental Health of Children and Youth in Ontario: A Baseline Scorecard.* Institute for Clinical Evaluative Sciences.

Perry-Parrish, C., Copeland-Linder, N., Webb, L., & Sibinga, M. (2016) "Mindfulness-based Approaches for Children and Youth" *Current Problems in Pediatric and Adolescent Health Care*, 46 (6), 172–178.

Ra, C., Cho, J., Stone, M., De La Cerda, J., et al. (2018) "Association of Digital Media Use With Subsequent Symptoms of Attention-Deficit/Hyperactivity Disorder Among Adolescents" *JAMA 2018*, 320(3):255–263. doi:10.1001/jama.2018.8931

Rizzolatti, G., & Sinigaglia, C. (2008) *Mirrors in the Brain: How Our Minds Share Actions and Emotions.* Oxford, UK: Oxford University Press.

Schonert-Reichl, K. A., Oberle, E., Lawlor, M. S., Abbott, D., Thomson, K., Oberlander, T. F., & Diamond, A. (2015) "Enhancing cognitive and social–emotional development through a simple-to-administer mindfulness-based school program for elementary school children: A randomized controlled trial" *Developmental Psychology*, 51(1), 52–66.

Semple, R. J., Lee, J., Rosa, D., & Miller, L. F. (2010) "A randomized trial of mindfulness-based cognitive therapy for children: promoting mindful attention to enhance social-emotional resiliency in children" *Journal of Child and Family Studies*, 19(2), 218–229.

Sibinga, E. M. S., Webb, L., Ghazarian, S. R., & Ellen, J. M. (2016) "School-Based Mindfulness Instruction: An RCT" *Pediatrics*, 137(1), 1–8.

Taren, A.A., Creswell, J.D., & Gianaros, P.J. (2013) "Dispositional mindfulness co-varies with smaller amygdala and caudate volumes in community adults" *PLoS One*, 8, e64574.

Waddell, C., Offord, D.R., Shepherd, C.A., Hua, J.M., & McEwan, K. (2002) "Child psychiatric epidemiology and Canadian Public policy: the state of the science and art of the possible" *Canadian Journal of Psychiatry*, 47(9):825–32.

Zelazo, P. D., & Lyons, K. E. (2012) "The Potential Benefits of Mindfulness Training in Early Childhood: A Developmental Social Cognitive Neuroscience Perspective" *Child Development Perspectives*, 6(2), 154–160.

Index